Make Your Brain Your B*tch

Mental Toughness Secrets To Rewire Your Mindset To Be Resilient And Relentless, Have Self Confidence In Everything You Do, And Become The Badass You Truly Are

REESE OWEN

© Copyright 2019 by Reese Owen - All rights reserved.

The following book is reproduced below with the goal of providing information that is as accurate and reliable as possible. Regardless, purchasing this eBook can be seen as consent to the fact that both the publisher and the author of this book are in no way experts on the topics discussed within and that any recommendations or suggestions that are made herein are for entertainment purposes only. Professionals should be consulted as needed prior to undertaking any of the action endorsed herein.

This declaration is deemed fair and valid by both the American Bar Association and the Committee of Publishers Association and is legally binding throughout the United States.

Furthermore, the transmission, duplication or reproduction of any of the following work including specific information will be considered an illegal act irrespective of if it is done electronically or in print. This extends to creating a secondary or tertiary copy of the work or a recorded copy and is only allowed with express written consent from the Publisher. All additional rights reserved.

The information in the following pages is broadly considered to be a truthful and accurate account of facts, and as such any inattention, use or misuse of the information in question by the reader will render any resulting actions solely under their purview. There are no scenarios in which the publisher or the original author of this work can be in any fashion deemed liable for any hardship or damages that may befall them after undertaking information described herein.

Additionally, the information in the following pages is intended only for informational purposes and should thus be thought of as universal. As befitting its nature, it is presented without assurance regarding its prolonged validity or interim quality. Trademarks that are mentioned are done without written consent and can in no way be considered an endorsement from the trademark holder.

ALL BOOKS BY REESE OWEN

Check out my other ebooks, paperback books, and audiobooks available on Amazon and Audible:

B*tch Don't Kill My Vibe
How To Stop Worrying, End Negative Thinking,
Cultivate Positive Thoughts,
And Start Living Your Best Life

Just Do The Damn Thing
How To Sit Your @ss Down Long Enough To
Exert Willpower, Develop Self Discipline,
Stop Procrastinating, Increase Productivity,
And Get Sh!t Done

Make Your Brain Your B*tch
Mental Toughness Secrets To Rewire Your Mindset
To Be Resilient And Relentless, Have Self Confidence
In Everything You Do,
And Become The Badass You Truly Are

REESE OWEN

Since you're my friend—we're friends, right??—I'd like to give you my audiobook (~~usually $14.95~~) for **<u>FREE</u>**.

Search for my name "Reese Owen" on Audible.

Audible member? Use a credit.
New to Audible? Get this audiobook **free** with your free trial.

REESE OWEN

CONTENTS

Introduction 1

Chapter 1: Change Your Mind 9

- ⇨ The Bullsh*t Illusion
- ⇨ The Real C-Word
- ⇨ Positively Brilliant
- ⇨ Are You The Bull Or The China?
- ⇨ Get Off The Couch Already
- ⇨ It Doesn't Make You Psycho
- ⇨ What Are You Looking At?

Chapter 2: Change Your Outlook 47

- ⇨ Sh*t Or Get Off The Pot
- ⇨ You Deserve Nothing
- ⇨ The Flipside Of Failure
- ⇨ You're Not That Special
- ⇨ Nothing New On Race Day
- ⇨ Don't Be A Whiny Little B*tch
- ⇨ "But" Nothing

Chapter 3: Change Your Focus 77

- ⇨ Success Is Freaking Boring
- ⇨ Quit Tripping
- ⇨ What You See Is Not What You Get
- ⇨ Make The Big Picture Bigger
- ⇨ Get Over It
- ⇨ Take The Wheel

Chapter 4: Change Your Habits   91

- ⇨ Snoozing Is For Losing
- ⇨ Zip Your Lip
- ⇨ You're Not Going To Like This
- ⇨ When Being Bad Is So Good
- ⇨ Everything In Moderation
- ⇨ Maybe You're A *Little* Special…

Chapter 5: Change Your Actions   109

- ⇨ Here We Go Again
- ⇨ Look In The Mirror
- ⇨ Chill Out, Bro
- ⇨ What On Earth Do You Mean?
- ⇨ You're A Joke
- ⇨ Who's To Blame?
- ⇨ Team Up

Conclusion   135

INTRODUCTION

Life is not a romantic walk in the park as you hold hands with destiny, giggle about the magical happenings of your day, and lick a shared ice cream cone, as you skip into the sunset, singing songs designed to be listened to by five-year-olds on long car trips. Life is tough, abusive, and sometimes downright cruel. Even so, you don't have to let life beat you down and take away all hope you have of experiencing something decent in the time that you put in on earth. It is possible to not have a wuss for a brain, take control of your mind, and therefore take control of your life, and make it into something that doesn't make you want to avoid all your high school reunions out of complete and utter shame.

Usually, I like to start by talking about a hypothetical person whose life is in hypothetical shambles, but this book hit particularly close to home, so at the risk of doing something that wouldn't at all surprise my mother, I'm going to start by talking about myself.

Looking back at how my life used to be, it was bad. I remember a few years back, I was sitting on the couch, feet up, probably wearing socks with sandals—I told you it was bad—gorging on my favorite meal, chips and dip—correction, *free* chips and *free* dip that I shamelessly took home from every restaurant I went to because I was that poor. Chip in my mouth, salsa dribbling down my lip, and TV remote in my hand, I mindlessly flipped through channels, hoping to land on a reality show that would show me people screwing up their lives so much that it made me feel better about my own. In other words, I was pissing away yet another day of my life, doing nothing.

This was pretty much the scene day in and day out. At the time, I thought there was nothing I could do to change the fact that I was working at a shit job and making next to nothing while I gave virtually everything I had just to keep myself from getting fired. And the sad thing is, as much as I hated the job I had at the time, I did want to keep it. Without it, then I would *really* be left with nothing. Right before this pathetic, free tortilla chips, socks with sandals phase of mine, there was an opportunity I was pursuing that didn't work out for me, and if I'm honest, looking back, I didn't have the resilience to keep at it and try harder. And as a result, I seriously thought that life was never going to get any better and that I was doomed to be some loser, perpetually on the couch, dressed like a hobo, and too lazy and defeated to actually go make something of my life.

In reality, I was not doomed to living this meaningless life where I wasted my days working for someone who couldn't even bother to remember how to spell my first name—my *one syllable* first name. I was just seriously whipped by my brain, that thought it was doing me favors by keeping me comfortable and cozy in the little hole I had dug for myself. By burying me into my metaphorical grave, my brain was able to protect me (and itself) from the serious energy it would take to shape up and ship out of this mess and get myself on track for a better life. And it would have taken *serious* energy. Socks with sandals, remember?

I don't recall exactly what I was doing when everything clicked into place, but I do clearly remember what it felt like to realize that the only reason I didn't have a better life was that I was too much of a wuss to make it happen. That's right, I wasn't the anomaly of the universe, the one unlucky person to have a black rain cloud following them around at all times, or the reason for the coining of the term "Murphy's Law." I was just too scared to get off my couch and try, because I feared rejection and defeat. It was time to make my brain my bitch, stop succumbing to the comfortable little rut it jammed me into, and start taking some responsibility for myself.

To be completely honest, after my initial epiphany over my level of pathetic-ness, I didn't immediately go from being too scared to make a change, to fierce and fearless lion ready to roar in the face of every challenge that tried to hold me back. I probably spent a good few months oscillating between the two. It was pretty embarrassing switching back and forth between these two states. Plus, it was exhausting getting seriously pissed off at myself every time I found myself engaging in old habits that kept me weak and useless. Even though I had the energy and desire to change my life, I was trapped under the quick whip of my ruthless brain. That's when I made it my mission to make a change in my life *for freaking real this time.*

When I realized that I was my own problem, I got out of my own way and started learning how to master my brain so that it wouldn't dare dream of holding me back from achieving success. Its mission was to keep me comfortable and its idea of comfort was sitting around earning a little more than minimum wage and complaining about the fact that I had to wait another thirty minutes for my pizza to arrive. Simply put, my brain was off its rocker, and I needed to give my own mind a piece of my mind.

The tips I am going to share with you in this book are the exact ones that I used to whip myself into shape, ditch the unhelpful, thoughtless habits of my weak brain, and teach both my brain and myself how to start living like the fierce lion I knew I was. By taking the time to actually read through and understand these tips, you can also whip your brain into shape and start taking action in your own life.

Now, I must warn you. Taking control over your brain is no easy feat. If you are truly serious about changing your life, you need to go ahead and commit to your change right now and hold yourself to that commitment for the rest of your life. This is like a marriage. You need to divorce your dysfunction, and get hitched to a whole new way of thinking and living. These principles may be quick and easy to read about in a few hours, but conquering them will take much much longer and be much much harder. If you truly want to be great, like, *Michael Jordan, Jeff Bezos* great, you have to implement everything you read about here into your day-to-day life. It is through action that change is achieved, not through reading and educating yourself and then carrying on with your lame life.

Implementation truly is the key difference between sucky, mediocre, and great people. Those who know that they want to make a difference in their lives and who are ready to start experiencing the greatness that they truly know they are capable of implement absolutely everything that they learn, allowing them to improve upon themselves over and over again. Before they know it, they are experiencing true greatness and it all happened because they were willing to learn, implement, and adjust their course of action as needed to keep them on the right path.

This is going to require a significant amount of mental toughness to keep you dedicated and confident throughout this entire process. Lucky for you, mental toughness is a cornerstone of this very book, as it has helped me immensely when it comes to truly changing my ways and sticking to my commitments even when I wasn't seeing results right away. Being able to stay resilient, consistent, persistent, and devoted to your path even when things don't seem to be happening the way you want is necessary if you are going to achieve changes in your life.

It was through mental toughness that Roger Bannister was able to break the 4-minute mile in 1954, through believing that he could and then staying resilient and consistent until he did. With that success under his belt, Bannister became one of the most memorable athletic runners of the 20th century. I guess it was kind of redundant and unnecessary there to call him athletic after I just said he did a 4-minute mile, but whatevs. You may not want to run a 4-minute mile, but you will need the same mental toughness that allowed Bannister to do it, if you are going to achieve your best life and achieve your own breakthrough.

Ready, future kings and queens of the jungle? Just so that I (and any people around you) know that you're serious, go ahead and let out your inner lion or lioness right now and *roar* out loud. Did you do it? I'm not sure if I hope you did or hope you didn't. But I do hope that you've made the definitive decision that it's time to start getting serious about your life and get okay with the fact that you are going to have to be okay with getting seriously uncomfortable until living on the edge of success becomes a thrill and living this "cozy" life you have been living seems horribly boring and pointless. So if you need to make like Katy Perry and roar out loud like a lion, no matter how silly it might look (or sound), you've proven to *yourself* (and everyone around you) that you have the cajones to actually make your brain your bitch.

Now that you have roared and shown your life and your neighbors just what you are made of, it's time for you to get started. I hope you are ready to make some radical changes in your life because once you finish reading this book and implementing all of the tools in it, life will never be the same for you again. Do you think you can handle it? I'll take that as a yes.

REESE OWEN

CHAPTER 1:

CHANGE YOUR MIND

If you truly want to whip your brain into shape and start taking control over your life, the first thing you need to do is change your mind. Until now, all of those thoughts you have been thinking in your life have done nothing more than lead to you feeling more hopeless than a kid who just found out that Santa isn't real.

Maybe you're miserable, your life doesn't look the way you want it to look, and nothing seems to be working out for you these days. Every time you look out into the world and on social media, you can't help but run into countless scores of people doing annoying things like smiling, celebrating their personal milestones, looking hot, and kicking butt. And you, well, you can't even remember the last time you smiled and it felt genuine.

The reason why your life seems so crummy is because…well, it is. And why is it that way? How did you end up being the unlucky person out of seven billion on this planet for whom nothing ever goes your way? Because you allow it. The reason why your life seems so crummy is that you have decided that living a crummy, half-assed, sorry excuse of a life is something that you are willing to endure. The fact that you keep seeing everyone else achieve great success while you sit around and continue watching crappy reality TV marathons, and muttering curses under your breath while eating last week's McDonald's leftovers has nothing to do with luck or fortune and everything to do with the way that you choose to see your life. In this chapter, I am going to show you how to change your mind so that you can stop settling for a life that is in desperate need for transformation and start working towards something truly meaningful.

The Bullshit Illusion

Your comfort zone is like a cozy, safe, and predictable little cocoon that you can curl up into any time you feel discomfort, allowing you to feel a sense of peace and relaxation in an otherwise chaotic world. Or at least, that's what you think your comfort zone is, which is the reason why you find yourself spending so much time pent up there, hiding away from the real world and real responsibilities. The truth is that your comfort zone is a bullshit illusion that you have fed to yourself in order to avoid the painful realities of what life truly is. In your comfort zone, you can pretend that you are doing everything you are supposed to be doing, when in reality you are hiding away from everything that you need to be doing. In your comfort zone, you can avoid the challenging conversations, the pressures of breaking your limitations, and the discomfort that comes with building a better life for yourself. Through that avoidance, although you gain an immediate sense of comfort in the short term, you create an even larger sense of discomfort in the rest of your life in the long term.

See, the comfort zone is a place that we tend to live when we need to feel like we have some form of control over our lives. I spent years tucked away in my comfort zone claiming that the only reason why I wasn't further ahead in my life was that I "didn't want to be," and not because I was too scared to actually get out and do anything about the things I hated in my life. From my comfort zone, I convinced myself that I was doing everything I needed to live a comfortable and safe life where nothing could hurt me or create any larger sense of pain. What I was actually doing was deluding myself into believing that I was feeling comfortable when, in reality, I was extremely disappointed in myself and in the "life" I had created for myself—or, rather, the life that I fell into as a result of my apathy and inaction.

I am willing to bet that if you were to look at your life right now, you would probably notice that you live in your comfort zone most of the time, too. No, I'm not necessarily saying that you *feel* comfortable; in fact, I know that you don't because one—the comfort zone *is* a bullshit illusion, and two—you picked up this book. What I'm saying is that you make the choices that seem to be the most comfortable based on all of the options that you think are available to you. And it is worth noting that no two comfort zones are alike. What's comfortable for one person may be uncomfortable for another, and vice versa. For this reason, the same exact action can be either comfortable of uncomfortable, depending on the person.

For instance, perhaps, instead of going out for a fun night on the town and enjoying fresh air and the comradery of good friends, you are cooped up in your house, watching *Fresh Prince* reruns just like you have been for the past ten years. Alternatively, maybe your problem is the exact opposite. Maybe you *are* out for a wild night on the town a little more than you would like to admit and you haven't been staying in enough to give yourself the chance to honestly address your life and take responsibility for the mess you have built for yourself.

See, living in your comfort zone seems great to you because the choices are familiar and the outcomes are predictable. But what actually ends up happening when you live in your comfort zone long-term is the exact opposite of comfort—it is complete and total discomfort. Yes, it feels good in the moment to skip preparing for that job interview and watch TV instead. But does it feel good to work a minimum wage job that you hate instead of one that pays you multiple six figures a year?

Operating from within your comfort zone brings no new opportunities for you to grow and achieve new things in your life. If you truly wanted comfort, you would think long-term and start making choices in favor of the *future* you like, I don't know, saving money or starting to pay off that student loan debt you've been bitching about that you've accumulated from the education you won't put to good use.

Getting uncomfortable now means that you get to experience a greater and more sustainable sense of comfort in the future. Which is why, right now, you are going to break the bullshit illusion of your comfort zone and get real on what will bring you *actual* comfort in your life. I want you to start by grabbing a journal, a piece of paper, a technological device with a screen and a keyboard, and writing down every single area of your life that makes you uncomfortable and then determine what familiar decisions you are making that keep you in that state of so-called "comfort." Then, I want you to determine what you could do differently that would support you in experiencing comfort for future you–regardless of what it feels like for current you.

For example, maybe you realize that you feel like a lowlife loser because you have no money saved and you have been living month to month in a basement for the past three years even though it was only meant to be a transition spot for you. But, you've managed to make this little dungeon basement feel like home, so the comfort of staying in a familiar place and going out every weekend to party and spend far too much money on booze has resulted in you being trapped in your transition and held back from moving forward as you originally intended to.

So, your action-plan for doing something different could be to go out less, stop paying for drinks, and start using that Grey Goose money for nest egg money instead so that you can save a dollar or two and move out of that grungy basement already and get yourself a real place—you know, the kind where you are actually *proud* to have people over instead of continually using excuses to get out of hosting weekly game night with your friends. *My landlord is renovating, so they pulled up the floors. They're repainting, and the smell has to dissipate. There's a noise ordinance for my building.* Bullshit. You live in some random old lady's moldy basement because you can't get your shit together.

The *Real* C-Word

If you truly want to make a change in your life, you need to embrace the *real* C-word—and not the one your douchebag uncle mutters under his breath when your mom takes the last dinner roll at Thanksgiving *again*. The real c-word that you need to be focused on when it comes to changing your life through your mindset is *confidence*. Truth be told, this c-word used to make me shake in my boots any time it came up.

I wanted to believe that I was confident and that I could do anything I wanted to, but when it came down to it, I had about as much confidence in myself as a dog owner has in their dog's ability to control itself around a freshly grilled T-bone steak. In other words, I truly believed that if I attempted to entrust myself with something as important as changing my life, that I would royally fail and be doomed to be a couch potato, destined to reside only in flophouses or moldy basements. I couldn't risk that, so instead, I simply sat around and let my life pass me by as I did nothing to try and improve upon it.

Wouldn't you know it, each day that passed by, nothing changed, and everything I was afraid of started falling into my lap as I watched my friends build their dream lives while I ordered yet another extra-large cheese and mushroom pizza from Greg, the Papa John's delivery guy I knew on a first-name basis. I saw Greg so often that Greg knew more about my life than some of my friends did. It was bad. And it got even worse when one day I ordered a pizza and saw that Greg was replaced with Adam, because Greg had gotten promoted. Even the pizza guy's life was looking up.

This was one of a series of moments that came together to prove to me that my lack of confidence would only continue to rob me of my future success if I never did anything to change it. One day, as serendipity would have it, I came across an old issue of Oprah's magazine, and in it, I found an article by Janine Latus that spoke on the importance of self-confidence and self-validation. Seeing her article made me realize that these were two things I struggled with big time. Greg wasn't the only person in food service I was on a first name basis with. Michelle, the Starbucks barista I saw every single week, consistently called me by the wrong name *every single time*. And for some reason, I just couldn't correct her. I truly felt that by speaking up for myself, even on trivial things, I was doing everyone a disservice and just making people's lives more complicated than they needed to be–including my own.

Come to think of it, one of the biggest tools I used to keep me from building my self-confidence was my comfort zone—the same one I just told you to kick in the 'nads and send packing. Unfortunately, I gained nothing when I lived in the shadows of confidence and shied away from the act of standing up for myself and validating my own desires, needs, and *self*.

Going back to Latus's article, she wrote about the importance of validating ourselves and how we often use mediocre excuses to attempt to justify why we continue to live our lives the way we do rather than facing the simple fact that we lack self-confidence. In her article, titled "Self-Esteem: The Repair Kit," she talked about how her own self-confidence was extremely low in high school and how she used flirting as a way to gain attention and feel good about herself. She also talked about how she would justify her excessive flirting habit by saying she was "simply expressing her sexuality, which is natural and healthy and right." She claimed that this habit carried on into her adult life as she continued to seek attention from those around her anywhere she would go. To Latus, any time she wasn't being told that she was attractive or wonderful, she felt like a total failure, and that's what really hit me.

I realized that one of the biggest reasons I lacked self-confidence in my own life was because I was afraid of doing everything wrong and not achieving the success that I desired for my life. For me, it was easier to watch my friends achieve everything I wanted even if that meant I was left in the dust, while I made excuse after excuse. I would tell myself lies like "I can't accomplish that" or "I don't *really* want that" or "I'd rather be humble than successful anyway," even when the reality was that I really did envy their success and want it for myself, but at the time I didn't know or believe that if I applied myself, I too could achieve it.

If you have ever heard of the idea of manifesting from anyone, you may have rolled your eyes and run other way before they pulled out their crystals and started telling you about their chakras, but consider this: we manifest exactly what we place our focus on. So, for me, by constantly focusing on thoughts like "I can't" or "I don't want to" even when I could and I did, I was manifesting a life filled with unfulfilled dreams and unmet expectations. The more I thought I couldn't do things, the less I tried, and the more I subconsciously further convinced myself of my own ineptitude, and I found things getting more and more difficult for me. The more I told myself I didn't want the things I truly did want, the less they presented themselves to me and the less I had the chance of making them happen.

I felt like I was in a funhouse filled with those crazy mirrors that constantly distorted my reality and emphasized all of the features I didn't want to be sharing with the world around me. The more I focused on these things, the greater they appeared, and the more challenging it was for me to accept where I was at in my life.

One of my favorite parts of Latus's article that really resonated with me back then was the part where she said she took a picture of herself, propped it up on a chair, and began talking to her picture about how she really felt. Initially, I admit it sounded like something only a bona fide psycho would do, but desperate as I was, the idea of emulating a bona fide psycho didn't scare me off. And lo and behold, I tried it, and it worked. The more I did it, the less I felt *One Flew Over The Cuckoo's Nest*, and the more I felt *Rocky Balboa*. I sat in front of a picture of myself and began to address every reason why I felt like I was inadequate or unworthy and I began verbally accepting myself for any shortcomings I felt I had, and telling myself why these shortcomings were either meaningless or imagined.

If you do this, you will likely find it to be quite an emotional experience that brings up pieces of your past that you thought you were done with for good. As I continued talking to my own face and expressing my current acceptance of myself and my desire to change my life so that I could begin experiencing more positivity, I felt things start shifting within me—not in the *I just ate a barbacoa burrito from Chipotle* way, but an actual mental and emotional shift.

I have to ask for your forgiveness in advance, as the next two minutes are about to get extraordinarily cheesy—like, Disney Channel original movie cheesy. But believe me when I tell you, as a result of this weird little exercise, the parts of myself that I had hidden and kept under wraps for so long were not only being exposed, but they were being accepted by the most important person in my life—myself.

Although I didn't walk away from that exercise every time with complete confidence, after repeatedly doing it, I did walk away with a solid foundation upon which my confidence would continue to grow over time. I felt as though I got to know myself in a brand new way and it became a lot easier for me to begin accepting everything about myself, including my true dreams and desires. For that reason, I highly recommend channeling your inner psycho, talking to your face, and spending time truly getting to know yourself so that you not only feel more confident in yourself, but also more confident in your decisions and your desires. This confidence will be the very foundation for making some real changes in your life.

Positively Brilliant

For years, I high tailed out of any situation where the words "think positive" came into play because I thought it was an exhausted avenue of bullshit that was used by cocky meditation gurus to try to banish rainy days and bounced checks. However, when I finally allowed myself to listen to, and understand, the value of positive thinking, I discovered that this is actually something that works, like a lot. If you are going to be lazy and only take one single thing away from this entire book (but please don't be *that* person) I would say take away the value of positive thinking and how you can literally think yourself into a better life experience.

Even if you're not the fluff type, just think about it—it makes complete logical sense. Your thoughts determine your beliefs. Your beliefs determine your actions. And your actions determine your results. If you don't believe that you can get that promotion, break that bench press record, or successfully start that business, then you can't. Good ol' Henry Ford, along with blessing us with the invention of the motor vehicle, also blessed us with a very well known, over-quoted quote—one that, surprise, I'm about to quote again: "Whether you think you can, or whether you think you can't, you're right." With positive thinking, comes positive action and positive results in your life. That's the good news. The bad news is that the inverse is also true. With negative thinking, comes negative action (which is actually usually just inaction or half ass action), and therefore negative (or no) results. If you are going to possess any level of mental toughness, ironically, you have to first embrace this "fluff stuff."

But, positive thinking is not just about painting the town positive, clicking your heels three times, and depositing your surprise check for $30,000 that came out of absolutely nowhere. In fact, positive thinking has absolutely nothing to do with any of that: positive thinking has more to do with your brain and your perception on life and the world around you than it does with anything else. The science behind positive thinking is fairly basic.

As a non-expert, and a non-scientist with zero credentials, allow me to explain the science of positive thinking to you. As far as science goes, any time you think positive and begin to expand your perception with positive thinking, you essentially build neural pathways in your brain that allow you to see and experience more positivity. The more you build and reinforce these neural pathways, the stronger they are and the more effective they become, thus making it easier for you to continue experiencing even more positivity in your life. Impressed? Not a bad explanation for a non-scientist with no credentials, huh?

Thinking positive thoughts doesn't only change your brain, though. It actually changes your entire life as a result of these actual physical changes. People who think more positively have been reported to improve their ability to think and analyze various situations, see their surroundings with a more optimistic perspective, remain more attentive to their environment, and experience a general increase in happy thoughts.

If you don't believe me, I encourage you to do a simple Google search about positive thinking and the impact that it has on your brain. Studies have been done by places like Kings College in London, the University of Kentucky, Harvard University, and John Hopkins Medicine, places that are all filled with actual scientists with actual credentials, and all proving that positive thinking can literally change your brain–and your life.

Just knowing that positive thinking is backed by so much science and has such a clear and specific method that works was enough to encourage me to stop being so Eeyore, and actually give it a try and see what it was all about. I used to be that friend that always had something negative to say about everything and everyone else outside of me. I hate her shoes, I hate his accent, her hair sucks, he can't actually be that happy with his girlfriend, love is for suckers. It was of course all just a reflection of how poorly I saw myself and felt about the state of my own life. And that constant negative thinking just weakened my brain down more and more, until the point where I didn't believe in anything, especially myself.

So, I did some research and I came across a book by Joel Osteen titled *I Am*. After gulping hard, taking in the fact that I'd gotten so low that I was actually considering reading a Joel Osteen book and taking it seriously, I dug into his book and discovered the power of the words "I am" and the power of positive thinking by extension. I began making simple changes, such as eliminating thoughts such as "I am so clumsy" or "I am too lazy" or "I am so fat from living off of tortilla chips and salsa for the past six months that the zippers on all my pants have now given up." And I started replacing those thoughts with thoughts like "I am mentally strong" and "I am motivated." I know, I know, repeating these hippy mantras is definitely on the fluffy end of the spectrum, but trust me, it works. These changes were minuscule, but they actually began having a huge impact on the way I thought and felt about myself and my life.

Suddenly, I was feeling a greater sense of energy and confidence when it came to trying new things, moving beyond my comfort zone, and making changes in my life. Where I used to see hopelessness or an endless number of humongous insurmountable obstacles, I was starting to see opportunities and believe that there was always a way around any apparent obstacle. Although I was not able to successfully convince myself that everything was now easy and all the things I ever hoped for would fall right into my lap, I did manage to convince myself that there was a solution to every problem and a way around every roadblock.

As cheesy as it may sound, I encourage you to embrace this simple saying: "positive energy, positive attitude, positive outcome." You don't have to light incense and bang a gong while chanting it aloud incessantly, but I do encourage you to repeat it in your head so you can begin to retrain your brain to think right thoughts. Then, begin looking for opportunities to make simple changes in your thoughts and attitude so that you can begin feeling a greater sense of positivity in your own life.

For instance, whenever a negative thought pops into your head, replay the saying in your head "positive energy, positive, attitude, positive outcome," and then consciously and deliberately reframe your original negative thought into a positive one. As you do, I encourage you not to expect massive miracles to take place, especially not overnight, however, instead look for the subtle yet powerful shifts that begin taking place. When you literally change your mind by increasing the number of positive neural pathways your mind possesses, it becomes a lot easier for you to see opportunities and develop the confidence to embrace them and truly begin changing your life.

Are You The Bull Or The China?

You have definitely heard the saying before: "Don't be a bull in a china shop." Or maybe you haven't. I actually hadn't until someone said it to me. Wait…that didn't really make sense. Well, actually, I guess it made perfect sense. I digress. Anyway, if you can imagine a gigantic raging bull in a china shop, you can probably infer the meaning behind the phrase, "Don't be a bull in a china shop." Well, I'm here to call bull-you-know-what on this one and tell you that it's time for you to be the bull, grab life by the horns, and start learning how to live your best life without being such a wimp about everything. See, we are raised to believe that acting big and bold is selfish or somehow wrong or arrogant, leading us to believe that we are "too much" for the world around us and that we have to play ourselves down just to fit into society.

Attempting to discard who you are in favor of being a member of society is painful and often damaging, but it is something we feel that we must do if we are going to fit in anywhere in life. So, we do it, and your brain does it to the best degree that it possibly can, ensuring that you relax your personality to the maximum degree. Which means that you begin to lack not only a sense of self, but also lack motivation, passion, and drive because you are now pursuing a life that no longer fits your energy in favor of one that allows you to fit into society.

Chances are that you have fit yourself into the cookie-cutter lifestyle so effectively that you fail to realize that you even do it anymore. You have grown so used to being the person that society wants you to be that you no longer recognize your laziness, passionless, and unmotivated lifestyle that is the unfortunate outcome of you trying to be the person who you thought you were "supposed" to be. Instead, you probably think it's just who you are or it's the way that life is supposed to be. I'm here to tell you that this is complete crap and that you are not meant to dumb yourself down to fit into a society filled with people who are too scared to see you for who you really are, and you are not meant to just sit on your hands, stifle your voice and your true ambitions, so as not to make too much of a fuss. Shifting out of this limiting perspective starts with you. You need to decide once and for all that you are done pretending to be a piece of china when you are, in fact, the bull who is ready to make a ruckus and shake things up.

In order for you to make this change, you need to decide that you are going to embrace confidence, eliminate your subconscious need to be accepted by society, and find your *true* self once again. If you want to be more fierce and confident like a bull, you need to rediscover that fire inside of you and learn how to bring your best, even under the pressure of everyone nudging you to slow down or conform to society's mediocre standards for "comfortable success." This requires you to know how to move forward even when you have all of the pressure of the world asking you to stop and stay quietly in your position so that you don't cause a scene.

As a side note, we all feel pressure at times, whether it's pressure to do greater or pressure to stay the same, or even the obvious pressure to perform successfully in a high stakes situation. But moving forward in the face of pressure is an essential skill for attaining personal greatness. Sometimes, you have to take inventory of what you are afraid of, give yourself permission to fail or be silly, and then have a blast becoming the real version of you. Pressure only matters when you are so afraid of failing that you can't move forward for fear of what you will think or of what other people may think if you don't come through. And guess who's the big loser in that scenario? That's right—you.

You are the one left there, restless and uncomfortable, wishing for a better life while you continue to succumb to the pressures of controlling other people's perception of you, and fulfilling the desires of other people to keep you in your nice, neat little box. The minute you give yourself permission to fail, permission to be disliked by others, and permission to do the things that light *you* up and make *you* happy, performing under pressure becomes significantly easier. This is because you have lifted the veil on your fear and given yourself full permission to charge forward anyway, true to your bullish nature.

In order for you to move forward like the fierce, fearless, confident human you were meant to be, you need to start by writing down a list of everything that has been holding you back. Write down every single worry, resource (or apparent lack thereof), internal factor and external factor that has been holding you back from achieving success or moving forward in your life. Now, take a reality check and address everything you've taken note of for what it really is—fear. Fear isn't real. It's just a thought. You don't have to believe all of the thoughts that go through your head. See your fears for what they are—fears, not facts, then, consider what ways you could take charge *right now* so that you can plow those fears out of your way and move forward, and commit to actually taking action on whatever your next step to greatness is, no matter how uncomfortable it may be.

Get Off The Couch Already

Are you still sitting on the couch right now, telling yourself that you will get up and start "soon," as if you actually will? Or have you actually gotten up and put some of these actions I've given you to work already? Are you telling yourself, "yeah, yeah, yeah, I'm sure that'll work for someone else, but it won't work for me"? Or are you telling yourself "yeah, yeah, yeah, I tried all that stuff before and it didn't work"?

If you have actually gotten up off your heinie and put actual effort towards making some changes in your mindset already, congratulations! You must really be ready to drop kick your unhappy life to the curb and get started with a new, fulfilling life. If you are still on the couch, however, and you've told yourself that you will start "just as soon as you get a journal" or "later,"

I see you, and I know you on a deep soul level. Because *I was you*.

I must have thumbed through, listened to, and scrolled by 793,868 empowering, uplifting, and inspiring tidbits before I ever actually got motivated enough to get up and do something. And let me tell you, when I did get up, it was reluctantly and I achieved next to nothing because my mind still wasn't in the right place. The truth was, I was anything *but* a self-starter. I had no idea how to motivate myself, I didn't know what it meant to take control, and I thought that changing my mind meant consuming every single piece of positive material I could get my eyeballs on, and letting it somehow do the work for me. What a load of crap.

It's not enough to have the mental strength to listen to some positive thinking recording. You have to muster up the mental strength to take action on what you hear. You can only educate yourself so much before you need to actually, you know, *do something with the knowledge*. Pro tip: sitting on your couch gobbling down another bag of chips and half-assed reading this as you binge-watch another show on Netflix absolutely does not count as having mental toughness, putting things into action, or making a change in your life. If you, like me, seriously suck at getting yourself up and motivating yourself to start making these important changes in your life, then you need to begin taking action on the following advice that I am going to give you.

This valuable piece of advice that I learned came from the National Strength and Conditioning Association (NSCA), an association responsible for training professional athletes and personal trainers. And if it's good enough for professional athletes and personal trainers, then it's good enough for me. What I learned, is that humans are motivated by one of two things. The first thing would be the motivation to avoid failure, and the second would be the motivation to achieve success. While we all possess both of these desires, each of us will be uniquely and more strongly driven by either one or the other. Rarely are we completely driven by both. By determining which one you are more focused on—achieving success or avoiding failure—you can begin creating a plan to help you motivate yourself.

According to the NSCA, learning how to motivate yourself to achieve higher and higher levels of success requires you to tailor your approach towards the specific type of motivation that you are most driven by. If you are more likely to be driven by a fear of failure, then you need to put pressure on yourself to begin changing your behaviors so that you do not become the failure that you are afraid of becoming. In other words, don't be afraid to play into your fear of failure to encourage yourself to see what you stand to lose (or unwillingly gain) if you do not make any changes in your life. If you are afraid of having people pass you by and achieve the success you always thought you would have while you sit around and do nothing every day, then motivate yourself by envisioning what your life might be like if you never change. Think of what your life would look like if you continued doing the same thing you are doing right now and stayed on the same path. Do you really want to be the one that no one hangs out with anymore because you are still living in an underground flophouse with three pieces of Craigslist furniture and rotten food in the fridge because you can't be bothered to shop, clean, or make a career?

Or do you want to be the person who is up there alongside your successful friends, living in a nice place, getting tagged on Instagram in exotic locations, and spending weekends attending thrilling events with people that you care about? For you, the best question to motivate yourself would be: "What do I stand to lose if I don't do this?" And if you're 100% honest with yourself, you know what your "this" is, so fill in the blank with whatever that thing is that you've been putting off or have been afraid of that you know can make a difference in getting you to your next level.

Now on the other hand, if you are motivated by the dream of future success as opposed to the nightmare of future failure, then you need to maintain a big, inspiring vision, keep it at the forefront of your physical and mental consciousness, and ensure that it aligns perfectly with your core values. Make sure that your dream is uniquely yours, not tainted in any way by any outside influence, and then remind yourself of this dream every single day to support you in getting off of the couch and making a change. Think about how much more you could have, or how much closer you would be if you were to get up and start making small steps towards your big dream today. Stay focused on the future, keep your dream personal and special, and make sure that you spend at least a few minutes per day envisioning your future and the success that you desire so that you can motivate yourself to keep moving forward. For you, the best question to motivate yourself would be: "What do I stand to gain if I do this?"

Either way, whether you are a fan of scaring yourself straight with the vision of yourself homeless under a bridge, or whether you prefer to maintain a more positive vision of yourself living the lifestyle of the rich and the famous, use the power of your vision to strengthen your mental will, and whenever you think of quitting or giving up, go back to your vision and allow it to give you the mental strength you need to push through to the other side.

It Doesn't Make You Psycho

You're not crazy if you talk to yourself. Well, maybe I should clarify here. You're not crazy if you talk to yourself and you're not yelling out loud in public having full-on conversation, adopting multiple characters and personas. Mental pep talks, however, are a great reason to talk to yourself, and really are essential for you to strengthen your brain and improve your quality of life.

You have heard it before and now you will hear it again—how you talk to yourself seriously matters when it comes to changing your mind and changing your life. People who consistently engage in negative self-talk will never have the life they dream of because they will always be stuck in a cycle of sabotaging their self-confidence and pushing the dream further away from them with each new put-down they tell themselves. Calling yourself a sissy-pants while you beat yourself up about ordering more takeout for dinner *(seriously, again??)* is not going to support you in actually getting yourself off the couch and moving forward towards a better life.

Perhaps, you're thinking, *But, I'm motivated by the idea of fear of failure. I need tough love. I don't like to coddle myself for unacceptable behaviors.* Even if you are motivated by avoiding failure, you need to be careful about the way in which you are talking to yourself so that your self-talk is actually productive and not destructive.

According to Toni Bernhard J.D. in her book *How To Be Sick*, she took a retreat in the late 1990s where a Buddhist teacher named Mary Orr told a story about feeling as though she had too much to accomplish and not enough time to accomplish anything. Orr told the members of the retreat that at one point she caught herself engaging in an internal dialogue that shocked her, especially since she knew she would never dream of speaking to anyone else in the way that she was speaking to herself.

While Bernhard claims that she could not remember the exact words of the story, she could remember the meaning behind it: how we talk to ourselves is often far harsher and less kind than we would ever talk to another human being. As a result, we inhibit our ability to achieve any type of success when it comes to our goals or life missions because we are constantly demeaning and degrading ourselves, chipping away at our self-confidence, self-esteem, and mental and emotional power. From within, we are tearing ourselves down to the point that we no longer possess the inner will or desire to move forward because we have been bullied (by ourselves) to the point of feeling as though we are not worthy nor capable of success.

Bernhard goes on to share an alternative from Buddhism: *metta,* or the act of building loving-kindness or friendliness in your life. According to Buddhism, *metta* starts within yourself and, from there, it cultivates and grows outward into your life. However, without first beginning with yourself, you would never be able to express loving-kindness and friendliness towards anyone because you are not experiencing it for yourself, either. In other words, "as within, so without" rings highly true in this scenario.

After reading this story about inner self-talk and taking a moment to really let it sink in, I realized that I was being pretty shitty to myself, to say the least. The number of times I would beat myself up for the life I was living and the names I would call myself were treacherous. Honestly, if someone else called me any of the names I called myself, I might have been ready to square off and show them a thing or two about who they were dealing with. Umm…can you say *unlike, defriend*, and *unfollow*? But me? I didn't have the balls to tell myself to take a hike and start treating myself better "or else." After all, what would my "or else" even be since it's not like I could square off with myself. Or could I?

The truth was I could, and as a matter of fact, I did. Of course, it wasn't like some epic brawl you see when two guys at a bar start arguing about sports or girls or whatever it is drunk guys argue about. It was quite different, yet it still had all the same impact as a good, strong right hook to the jaw.

It looked something like this: I stood in the mirror, staring at myself and thinking about all of the names I had called myself over the years and all of the ways I had treated myself that I wouldn't dare do to another person or let another person do to me. Then, I realized three things. The first thing is that I had gotten so lazy that my mirror needed some serious Windex because it was so dirty that I could barely see my recently developed fat rolls. The second thing I was thinking was that I'm pretty messed up in the head and unkind and I had some serious shit to figure out. And the third thing that came to mind was that most of these negative voices were never even mine to begin with. They were a mixture of voices that I had adopted over the years after being called various names and told various things from others in my life.

Like that one time a bully in high school called me buck-toothed or when my Mom said my hair never sat right and I looked like a worthless bum who would never amount to anything. Yeah, she wasn't very nice. But, these voices never came from me. They were the unkind words of everyone else I'd encountered along my life journey, and they morphed into one voice that sounded a lot like mine, but in reality, it was nothing I would ever purposefully say to myself.

And it makes total sense. I'm no baby scientist or anything, but I don't think babies come out of the womb self-deprecating themselves and constantly calling attention to everything that's wrong with them. *Ugh, my head is lumpy and soft. Look at these gross fat rolls on my legs. Geez, I desperately need to style this hair. My stupid neck and spine, can't even hold my head up right.* But as we grow and get further and further into life, we meet other humans that send us messages either consciously or unconsciously about how we are inferior. And eventually, we start to believe them, positive or negative. Unfortunately, we are often fed with more negative than positive.

It's all happening underneath: in your subconscious layer. Recognizing these negative words I'd unknowingly carried with me, and the pain that they were bringing me shed a lot of light into my life and into the reasons why I was still glued to the couch, despite trying to get up numerous times to try and engage in some life-changing activities. Still, the realization itself did not feel like enough to actually make a change and start treating myself better, so I kept talking to myself like I was the scum of the earth for a while longer.

It wasn't until one day I was thinking some particularly harsh words, and suddenly, I remembered my face in the dirty mirror looking back at me (well, as best as I could through the dust that had accumulated on the surface of the mirror), and my immediate thought was "*I would never say any of this to a child.*" For some reason, thinking of the child version of me, being told all of these negative things was enough to get me to stop. It was around that time that I started to become more self-aware over my daily thoughts and I started to disown all the negative voices that would pop into my head. If I wanted to have any hope of regaining control over my mind to regain control over my life, I was going to have to eliminate those negative voices and restore my compassionate inner voice. Once I made that decision, everything changed.

In order for you to truly motivate yourself into action and start getting the positive results you want, you need to stop calling yourself a whiny little cry baby or a worthless couch potato and start telling yourself that you are capable and worthy. As you do, those positive neural pathways that we talked about will begin forming in your brain, creating an actual physical opportunity for change directly in your mind.

Another bonus: you will also start to experience a more peaceful inner environment that supports you in living a stronger and more positive life. *That* is the environment that you need in order to have a strong, resilient mind, and to begin thriving and building success in your life, rather than lounging around doing more nothingness on top of the nothingness you have already accomplished in your recent past.

You can start right now by doing exactly as I did: Go in the mirror (maybe make sure it's clean first) and begin to recall some of the names you have called yourself and some of the abusive things you have said to yourself in the past. Then, think about where these thoughts and names *really* came from and how you actually feel every single time you hear them, especially from yourself.

Once you've done that, start making a conscious effort to notice the times where you begin thinking these thoughts in your daily life and then think about how they are making you feel or how they are influencing your active behaviors. Chances are, you will realize that they are influencing you to slow down, stop what you are doing, stop believing in yourself, and resume your typical habits of doing abso-freaking-lutely nothing. After you see just how negative of an impact these thoughts are having, you can start focusing on replacing them with thoughts of acceptance, approval, compassion, and empathy for yourself.

What Are *You* Looking At?

According to Ph.D. Frank Niles, a social scientist and life and business strategist, visualization is one of the most powerful practices you can use if you want to achieve your goals and make changes in your life. When it comes to the human brain, attempting to create something that you have never actually seen before is challenging because your brain cannot "see" what the end goal is. As a result, it does not know what to work towards and it struggles to motivate you and your actions to drive you towards achieving your dream or vision. The old saying "you must see it to believe it" truly does matter when it comes to getting your brain on board and rewiring it for the success that you seek.

As I was reading through his work, what really stood out to me was that Niles emphasized the science and psychology behind visualizing your dreams into reality. This made a lot more sense to me than the "think it and you will be it" crap that self-proclaimed gurus kept posting all over social media as they tried to peddle their $200 self-help courses to unsuspecting, vulnerable individuals. Unlike those, which often came in 3-step "solutions" that were barely explained, Niles explained visualization in a way that proved to me that this stuff actually works. The way he explained it was using the performance of athletes and how visualization changed the way athletes could improve their performance and achieve higher success. According to some of the studies Niles read, in using visualization in addition to actual active practice, athletes were able to improve their coordination, concentration, motivation, and confidence.

The more I dug into this theory, the more I realized that it really did go a lot deeper than those bullshit 3-step guides I was being shown time and again with the same recycled information and a mountain of inbox spam that inevitably followed. Instead, I discovered that your brain actually does not fully comprehend the difference between things that you see in real life and things that you visualize in your brain.

That's why many times if you wake up in the middle of a dream it takes you a while to convince yourself that the dream wasn't a part of reality. In my case, this unfortunate circumstance often took the form of me begrudgingly waking up, devastated when I came to the realization that I wasn't actually an instantaneous multi-millionaire, married to Jake Gyllenhaal, and driving a Rolls Royce to the Whole Foods store off of Rodeo Drive every Saturday morning. Snapping back from *that* reality was always a *serious* bummer.

When you incorporate visualization practices in your life, you essentially teach your brain about an alternate reality that you wish to exist, and your brain begins to accept this alternate reality because it can "see" it, therefore it believes it to be true. What ends up happening is that your brain performs exactly as it would if you were actually living out the reality that you were holding onto in your head. New neural pathways are created and your brain begins to tell your body to "perform" in line with your new visualized habit, action, or lifestyle, even though you are not yet physically performing the habit or living the lifestyle. As a result of this mimicked mental experience, you can mentally experience similar results from thinking things into existence as you can by actually implementing the steps of putting them into existence.

This does *not* mean that you can sit around on your couch and watch *Looney Toons* all day while you sip on orange juice and visualize thousands of dollars piling into your lap. Doing that is just going to keep you in the exact same horizontal position on your couch that you have already found yourself stuck in, and it may even make you more depressed when it inevitably doesn't work and you feel like, once again, there's something wrong with you.

Instead, you need to use visualization in addition to actual productive action. When their powers combine, you allow yourself to visualize change happening in your life and mentally prepare for it by creating the new neural pathways that you will need to make said changes a reality. It's essential that you follow those visualizations with intentional action so that you can begin taking the necessary steps toward building your success.

With the combination of both visualization and physical action, your brain will have a jump-start in producing the pathways required to help you achieve the success you desire, meaning you will get there a whole heck of a lot quicker. This is far more productive than trying to bully yourself into success, only to find yourself feeling too defeated and too depressed to actually make any changes in your life. Beating yourself up is a surefire way to kill your drive, weaken your mind, and shortcut your way to failure.

So, make sure to incorporate visualization into your daily life, and use it to your benefit. And as an added bonus, just like holding on to the vision of the future successful or future unsuccessful you can be enough to make your mind strong enough to motivate you, visualization has a similar power. Visualizing yourself being the person you want to be and having the life that you want to have will give you the strength to push through those difficult mental barriers when times get tough and things don't seem to be going your way.

In order to begin building a strong visualization for yourself and making positive changes in your life, you need to start by getting clear on what it is that you want to visualize into your reality. Start by thinking long-term, and then consider what it would take to get there. For example, if you want to be working in a far better job and making more money but you struggle because you lack confidence, then you may want to begin by visualizing yourself as a more confident person. But don't just think about it—remember to actually *visualize* it. See yourself with your head up, shoulders back, strutting down the street in a killer outfit, talking confidently to a room full of people completely engrossed in what you're saying, really see what you as a confident person actually looks like.

By regularly visualizing yourself as someone who has confidence, you will find that it becomes much easier for you to actually experience and exhibit confidence when it comes to doing things in your life. Then, you can continue visualizing yourself down the path to success until you inevitably reach it in the end.

CHAPTER 2:

CHANGE YOUR OUTLOOK

How you feel about yourself and the way you choose to engage with the world around you is only the first part of achieving some form of control over that unruly brain of yours. If you truly want to make your brain your bitch, you also need to change the way you perceive the world around you and the beliefs and opinions that you have over everything in your life. By changing the way you see the world around you and choosing to see it for what it truly is instead of what you have believed it to be for all these years, you improve your ability to actually interact with the world in a way that moves you forward.

In this chapter, we are going to address how *you* see *your* world, and how that perception literally shapes the way you interact with everything in your circle of existence. By getting a clearer perspective on the world and choosing to adopt a perspective that is empowering and motivating, you can completely change the way you address your life and how you proceed down the path of success. As you enforce these steps, you will discover that not only does the way you carry yourself and manage yourself change, but the way you gain value from the world around you changes, too. These are the actions that you need to take if you want to stop feeling like a little bitch that has been victimized by the world and instead feel like a fierce lion or lioness who is totally in charge of this whole thang.

Shit Or Get Off The Pot

If you are going to truly change your life, you need to "shit or get off the pot." It's as simple as that. Either begin doing what it takes to succeed, or stop pretending that you ever intended on doing something meaningful in your life and just give up for real. Give all the way up. That also includes giving up complaining about the changes you haven't seen in your life or the results you don't have. Can I tell you a secret? You don't have the results you want to have because you won't do the things you don't want to do.

And if you're not going to do what it takes, don't. And if you are, then do. That simple.

Motivating yourself and getting your mind on board with creating success in your life is one half of the battle, but you cannot solely rely on your motivation and willpower to keep you moving forward. Motivation and willpower are merely the momentum that will keep you in motion, but if you do not have any sense of direction or focus, you will never actually achieve anything. Instead, you'll end up getting bored and will likely find yourself succumbing to the very same habits that you are trying to eliminate from your life right now.

See, adjusting your mindset and building up the motivation to head onwards is powerful, and it gives you what you need to actually get out there and make something of your life. This is like putting your foot on the gas and feeling that rev of the engine as your car begins moving forward. However, if you do not continue giving your car gas and giving it direction by steering, you are never going to get to your desired destination because your car has no idea where on Earth it is supposed to be going. Instead, you will probably just crash into something and experience a severe blow to your momentum that knocks you down on your ass and keeps you horizontal on the couch for another decade or two. Metaphorically speaking, of course, since you are not actually going to go out and drive your car straight into an obstacle.

The act of giving yourself direction and actually feeding yourself the knowledge you need to advance in your life relies on you making commitments and then actually seeing your commitments through *every single time*. No more making a commitment to do something and then saying you'll get to it tomorrow, and then six years from now reminiscing on that day as you reflect on your unchanged life and shrug your shoulders at your failures. No. Just, no. This time, when you say you are going to do something, you are going to actually begin making the necessary adjustments in your life *immediately* so that you can move forward with your changes and create some serious success in your life.

If you've read my other book, *Just Do The Damn Thing*—cough cough, wink wink, nudge nudge—then you already know that one of my favorite tools that really helped me change my act and begin actually taking action when I said I would was reading Mel Robbins' book *The 5 Second Rule*. In that book, she mentions the importance of taking action immediately before your brain moves on to another thought and forgets about the original one entirely.

I wasn't surprised to learn that we think between 50,000 and 70,000 unique thoughts per day, but I was surprised to learn that most of these thoughts are completely forgotten about within moments. I realized that a large part of why my motivation was not enough was because I wasn't actually using it to get moving. It was like pushing on the gas while my car was still in park. It'll make a lot of noise, but it won't ever actually move. That was me, telling everyone who would listen (from my couch, of course) about how successful I would become and about how many changes I would see in my life only to follow my wild sense of motivation with the words: *"Ehhh...I'll start tomorrow"* or *"I'll do it later."*

If you truly want to step into action, I suggest taking Robbins' approach and implementing the 5-second rule into your own life. The minute you come up with an idea that you know is going to help you advance towards your goals in life, act on it within 5 seconds. If you need to, do exactly as Robbins does and countdown to yourself: "5... 4... 3... 2... 1... blast off!" And then immediately begin taking action that gets the wheels spinning on your new idea. This could be anything from booking an appointment to making a life-changing call or investing in a new stock or index fund. Just make sure you do something immediately that gets you a solid step closer to doing something valuable that in the long run is well worth your time and cold hard moola.

By jumping into action immediately and putting something into motion that supports your ultimate goal, you turn your idea into a *plan,* a now executed plan at that. Now that your momentum has been directed in a productive way and is moving toward something real and meaningful, you can feel certain that you are going to be able to take serious action toward your incredible dreams, and if you continue doing so, you will see them come to fruition. You're training your brain not just to think, but to *act* on your thoughts. And to take it a step further, you're training your brain to act regardless of your feelings. None of this *"I don't feel like it"* or *"I'm tired"* crap. You control your brain, instead of letting your brain control you.

This is the key to making sure that you actually follow your commitments through no matter what. It will be challenging, obstacles will arise, and you will find yourself feeling persuaded back into your old habits of doing nada. But you need to drag your ass kicking and screaming into actually doing what you know you need to do and what you say you're going to do. The more you practice staying committed, the easier it will be for you to remain committed to pursuing future goals and the more likely you will actually move towards making the items on your fabulous vision board a reality.

You Deserve Nothing

One reason why your brain is all whiny and weak may be because you think for some reason that you're entitled to something. Get inside your head that you have to work for *everything*, and maybe then, you wouldn't be so quick to whine and complain and feel sorry for yourself every time something doesn't automatically go exactly your way.

Remember that old coot that's always bitching and moaning about how the new generation is entitled, lazy, and thinks the world owes them something? That old coot was onto something. That old coot knows what it actually takes to turn a life into something meaningful that's worth living. Sure, maybe we can blame the older generation for melting the economy, depleting our future social security, ruining the job market, killing the earth, and otherwise causing us to inherit complete chaos and filling our minds with outdated rules on how the world works, but the older generation had it seriously right when they said that entitlement is *not* a virtue. Running around believing that the world owes you something is going to leave you feeling like an unpaid debt collector with no one to actually collect debts from because, news flash buddy, no one owes you a damn thing.

If you want to achieve something in your life, you need to stop pretending that things are going to fall into your life because you inherently deserve everything that you ask for and you don't need to do anything to actually, you know, *earn it*. This isn't sixth grade and you are not shouting at your Mom to bring you a peanut butter and jelly sandwich while you attempt to beat the first level of *Super Mario*. No, it's going to get a lot harder than that to get what you want. This is adulthood, my friend, and let me tell you the challenges and rewards are not nearly as simple as they were back in those days. Your real life is more like the *tear-your-hair-out* impossible level *The Perfect Run* in *Super Mario Galaxy 2*.

If you want to achieve anything in your adult life, you need to embrace the fact that it is going to take time, work, and serious effort on your behalf. That does not mean your entire life is going to be a back-breaking, incessantly laborious chore that has you crawling into your bed weeping for mercy every single night, although it will definitely feel like that at times. But, it does mean that there will be periods where you are going to be at it twenty-four hours a day, working towards your new life around the clock and doing everything it takes for you to succeed. You do not get even a minute off unless you want your old habits to creep in and cause you to find yourself succumbing to the nothingness that you have grown used to all over again.

Overcoming entitlement is not just about realizing that no one in this world owes you a single thing, though. Believe it or not, entitlement mentality is a real thing and if you believe that everyone owes you something, chances are, you are a victim, my friend. You are actually suffering from this in your own life. The way that you can overcome your entitlement mentality starts with you getting out of your own head and seeing the reality of the world that lies around you.

You need to talk less and listen more, pay more attention to others in this world and recognize the people around you, and show respect to people in the same way that you want them to show respect to you. If you want to seriously make a change in your life, you need to start seeing the reality that you and everyone around you are one and the same. Yeah, I know you are special and unique because you won the participation award in the Middle School Spelling Bee, and your Mom fluffed your hair and called you her little snowflake all the time, but that doesn't mean that you are *more* special than anyone else. It also doesn't mean you are any less special, because we are all the same level of specialness, and we are all entitled to receiving the same level of absolutely freaking nothing like the rest of the world is. Doesn't that make you feel better?

RANDOM, YET HELPFUL SIDE NOTE:

Once upon a time, I was on my high horse. When I finally mustered up enough of a fire in me to escape the butt ruts I'd left in my couch after months and years of sedentariness, my pride and my ego in unison told me that I was going to figure this thing out alone and do it all myself. But, as I got closer and closer to my goals, I found that it got harder and harder to "level up" and takes things to that next level of success. Then, one day, I came across an African proverb—yes, that happens to me all the time—and its message really resonated with me. *If you want to go quick, go alone. If you want to go far, go together.* When I first read this proverb, I realized that I had been working tremendously hard to get ahead in life by doing everything on my own and discrediting the value that other people's contributions could have in my life. So, naturally, I was left trying to do everything alone and I received as little as I gave. In the end, I hit a wall, and got to a place where I couldn't go any further because I simply didn't have what it took to get anywhere meaningful all by myself.

When I realized that I couldn't do it alone like I originally thought and wanted to, I hopped off my high horse—and let me tell you, it was a long way down—and started recognizing that I was not the only person with good ideas. I needed to tap into other people—peers, mentors, coaches—for their guidance, knowledge and expertise. When I did that and made that change, my life did too.

AND NOW, BACK TO OUR ORIGINALLY SCHEDULED PROGRAMMING:

Remember, everyone is equally important and we all deserve to have good things in our lives. The way to go about getting those good things isn't to wait for other people to do all of the hard work for us and hand us what we want, but instead to do the work for ourselves and expect for good things to happen as a result. When you do good things and experience good things, a wonderful type of energy shift begins to happen in your life, too.

As a result of all of the great things you are offering to the world around you, more great things come your way. In the end, you begin receiving more from others because you are also giving more to others, creating an equal and positive balance of receiving and giving that leads to many great things coming your way, and going towards others, too. This type of balance and community leads to many empowering and positive changes, so I highly recommend you start taking advantage of this tip in your own life as soon as possible. You can start by getting up off your couch right now and making some positive changes in your life that will benefit yourself, as well as those around you. Believe me when I say that you will feel *ah-mazing* when you start taking responsibility for your life and seeing everyone, including yourself, winning as a result.

The Flipside Of Failure

The fear of failure can be a crippling, terrifying, seriously intense kick in the crotch for anyone who has no idea how to overcome this fear. Personally, my fear of failure was so massive that I felt literally paralyzed from acting on any of my desires, in case I wouldn't be able to actually make them come to life. In those moments where I did feel that I would be able to bring them to life, I would give it the old heave-ho, only to find myself backing out and quitting at the first sign of failure or rejection. I was seriously terrified of not being able to get what I wanted, so instead, I foolishly sat back and pretended that I didn't actually want it in the first place. I thought that if I pretended as much, I would certainly be able to overcome the deep yearning for something more and grow to become intensely satisfied with my lame-sauce lifestyle. It never happened.

Instead of finding myself contented with doing virtually nothing, I found myself depressed that I was stagnant. The lack of activity in my life and my lack of drive to move forward due to the intense fear of failure kept me unwilling and unable to build the skills I needed in order to do anything meaningful or progressive. I started to feel like a little senior citizen sitting in my little senior home perched on my little couch, with my little friends Agnes and Mildred, complaining about everything that happened (or didn't happen), and just waiting for death to call. And, sadly, it's not like this vision was that far off. I was doing nothing with my life, so essentially all I was doing was waiting it out until it was over.

The fear of failure is a crippling fear that can keep you living in a chronic loop of negative beliefs, awful self-talk, and an unwillingness to move forward for fear of looking silly in front of others. And the irony is, while you're afraid of looking bad in case you fail at pursuing something, it's not like you're giving off mega success vibes, so you already look pretty bad and pretty silly, seeing as how you're already a failure when you're at the pinnacle of your low point.

At the time, I probably would have never admitted to the fact that it was my fear of failing that kept me from moving—especially after I realized that a fear of failure was an excuse, and completely backward since a fear of failure means you have already failed. Think about it, if you are so afraid of not achieving your dreams that you keep yourself small and feed into your fear of failure by doing nothing, then what are your odds of actually making your dreams come true? *Zero.* Your chances are the absolute lowest when you let a fear of failure drive you, even if you try and fool yourself and others into believing that the real reason why you are not acting on any of your desires is that they "don't exist."

Over the years, I've learned that a fear of failure often arises from a fear of the short-term outcome if we are unable to achieve our desired results. For example, say your big picture goal is to get a new fancy schmancy job. So, the first step? Job interviews. You set the intention to totally nail an interview for said new job and then during that job interview, everything that could go wrong does. You arrive late because of construction, your outfit looks like a toddler dressed you because there was a problem at the dry cleaners, and you give odd, side-eye inducing answers for every question you are asked because you are overly stressed and anxious. The interview goes so bad that it feels like something they could air on *American's Funniest Home Videos* and you might actually win an award for it.

But at the time, what you don't realize is that just because there are mini failures along the way to your goals, it doesn't disqualify you from the ultimate success you're seeking down the road. Bombing one job interview or looking like a complete idiot at one career networking event doesn't mean that you will never land that dream job. But, if you are suffering from a fear of failure, an embarrassing experience (or the idea of enduring one) might be so crippling that you might make a declaration to never attend another interview or try for a new job ever again because the humiliation is just way too bad. This is because your primary focus is on the short-term embarrassment, the fact that you did not get that one job you wanted, which then leads to drawing the incorrect conclusion that this job will not be the path to all of the success that you have secretly been dreaming of when you cry yourself to sleep every night.

If instead of focusing on those challenging bits, though, you were to turn your freaking head and look in the other direction, you might see this entire experience as one fortunate opportunity to support you in landing a way better job in the future. Rather than wallowing in self-pity over who-knows-how-many glasses of wine, you could take a moment to consider the opportunity for growth here.

Maybe there was something that could have been done to prevent you from being late. Waking up earlier, perhaps. Charging your phone overnight so your battery doesn't die and your alarm goes off. Looking up the parking situation the day before so you know to go to the ATM and get cash for parking now. Looking at the traffic alerts in the morning so you know to avoid the freeway because of the giant Ramen noodle spill. And maybe it would have been a good idea to have a backup outfit available for the meeting, or to have picked up your dry cleaning a few days earlier so that there would have been plenty of time to sort out your mishaps.

Maybe instead of wallowing in self-pity and misery over the fact that you did not get the job and are now doomed to minimum wage employment for the rest of your life, you could work to prepare yourself better for next time, whether that means planning out your outfit and other logistics in advance, or practicing interview questions so you're better able to answer questions under pressure and nail it even if you are feeling stressed and anxious about the whole ordeal. Maybe, you know, you could make a *change* so that you could start experiencing more positive results in your life. Or, you could just sit there and down another pizza and let yourself waste away another decade of doing absolutely nothing if that's what you would rather do.

If you are smart and you truly want change in your life, however, then it's time that you start putting some boundaries around how you are willing to let your failures define your life. You need to start acknowledging the fact that failure sucks and that dealing with it is painful, but whether you like it or not, it is an inevitable fact of life and any time you attempt to make changes, you are going to embrace varying degrees of failure. For me, it came down to weighing my options: continue feeling like a failure while I waste my life away and achieve nothing, or work my ass off while I make my brain my bitch and endure moments of failure as well as everlasting periods of success. Obviously, I chose the moments of failure on my way to ultimate success over the constant feeling of being a worthless little weakling who would never amount to anything.

Here's how I did it.

I started by realizing that failure was going to hurt whether I liked it or not, but that it didn't have to linger for so damn long if I didn't want it to. I set a new rule that I was not going to allow myself to wallow in self-pity for any longer than I needed to, so I had a time frame: I gave myself 24-hours to wallow over failures that were smaller and 48-hours to wallow over ones that were larger. After that time frame, I was still allowed to feel the failure if it was still bothering me, but I was not allowed to continue sitting around doing nothing about it and letting it eat away at me. I had to get back on the horse, try another way, and start moving forward again into my next order of business.

Once my time period was up, I would assess my failure and consider how it may have been caused by my own actions and behaviors. I would also consider anything that may have been beyond my control and let myself off the hook so that I stopped holding myself in a state of paralysis for things that truly were not my responsibility. For the things I was in control over and that I could change, I would take the time to consider a new approach, and then I would do my best to implement that new approach going forward. By seeing my failures as lessons and showing a willingness to learn from them and improve on myself, I was able to whip my brain out of the negativity loops and find myself seeing opportunity and lessons in *everything*. Naturally, because I was open to learning more, I *did* learn more and I was able to make something out of those experiences: *success*.

You're Not That Special

How many times have you taken things personally, heard criticism and thought it was feedback, tried to improve yourself so that you suited other people's needs, or stopped doing what you were doing because someone else told you it was stupid or a waste of time? Most of us can confidently say that we have engaged in these unhealthy, self-sabotaging behaviors *many* times in our lives. We have a tendency to want to fit into our groups, social circles, and society so badly that we genuinely believe that everything we are told needs to be taken personally, internalized, and improved upon in order for us to fit in anywhere.

What ends up happening instead is that we are far too malleable and we start making unnecessary changes and "improvements" on ourselves to fit in with groups that we don't even truly care about. In the end, we become so detached from who we are that we cannot even recall what it is that we want or what changes we want to make in our lives, and then enters the frustration, and soon after, the depression.

Right before I engaged in my hiatus where I hid out in my apartment and ate Cheez-Its and watched reruns for several months on end, I remember feeling a deep sense of frustration because I didn't believe I fit in anywhere. I thought I was the only person in the world who could not seem to "get it right" and fit in with a group of people and keep myself on a clear and straight path towards my desires. Heck, my desires changed every time someone told me what I *should* be working towards or what I *should* be avoiding in my life. It was insane the amount of "phases" I went through, just trying to gain the approval of other people in my life so that maybe I could stop being such a loser and just fit in already.

The truth is: you are *not* that special, none of us are. Most of the people who give you feedback or criticize you in your day to day life mean absolutely nothing, and they should have absolutely no impact on who you are or who you choose to become in life. Even your well-meaning Mom or your Grandma who constantly critiques your wardrobe and your accommodations don't actually care about the things they complain about as much as you think they do. I mean, do you think your Aunt Rose actually spends countless hours on the couch in a constant state of severe panic, worrying about that awful dinner you made six years ago when you attempted to cook on Thanksgiving? No, your Aunt Rose does not give one crap that your food could easily be out-performed in a taste test by a McRib. I promise.

Taking everything personally in your life is not only exhausting, but it is holding you back big time. Your constant need for the approval of everyone who crosses paths with you is going to leave you feeling as though you can never do anything right in your life and like your desires and dreams are meaningless because they will never come true anyway. And they won't, at least not with that attitude. Instead of searching for constant approval and making far too many changes to your life, keeping yourself in a non-stop identity crisis, you need to start considering who you are and what you want in your life. You know, the you that you would be if you didn't give one single shit about what anyone else thought about you. *That* version of yourself.

Detaching from criticism and not taking things so personally means that you need to learn how to appreciate what others say without internalizing it and feeling the immediate pressing need to completely change everything about yourself. Even though it feels good, you will also need to detach from the praise given to you by others because your constant search for approval is just as dangerous as your constant avoidance of negative feedback. The best way to do this is to begin remembering that feedback belongs to *other people,* not you. When you receive feedback, this tells you something about the other person and their preferences, not you and yours. This is just a reflection of that person and their beliefs, opinions, and perception, it truly has absolutely nothing to do with who you actually are or what you need to do in your life to be "worthy."

This does not mean that feedback isn't important. Constructive feedback that resonates with you and actually fits with your desired path can be extremely helpful. Don't be so entitled as to think that you are the only person whose doo-doo don't stank, because believe me, it does. It *is* crap after all. Knowing how to identify feedback that can actually be constructively applied to your life so that you can improve upon yourself and experience real, positive change is a valuable tool to have.

The best way that you can do this is hear feedback, consider if it actually applies towards your dreams (since you are the only one who knows what they are), consider the source (automatically discredit anyone who is perpetually miserable, negative, and unsuccessful), and then choose to act on it in a meaningful way *if* it does actually apply to you. For anything that doesn't apply to you, a polite nod will suffice as a response. Then get the heck out of there. You don't need your mind, energy, emotions, or consciousness muddled with things that are not in alignment with your values and desires, so no need to continue soaking in information and feedback from people that is in contradiction to what you want and need.

Nothing New On Race Day

I love sports analogies and references to professional athletes when it comes to matters of mental toughness because athletes need an extraordinary amount of mental strength to achieve the things they do in the field, on the court, or in the weight room. Applying those same principles outside of the field, the court, or the weight room, has a tremendously positive impact on other areas of your life. Professional athletes have a saying they use: *Nothing new on race day*. This saying refers to the fact that the athlete has prepared for their upcoming event for so long that they know exactly what to expect, and even the "surprises" that pop up are not that surprising to them. They are so prepared for what's at hand that they know how to move forward with grace no matter what may arise, thus cementing in their likely chances of winning at anything they set out to accomplish. When I first heard of this motto, I was actually deep in the process of learning about analysis paralysis and how our constant need to know everything can lead to us being unwilling to move forward because we feel like we don't yet know enough to make the right move.

Nothing new on race day to me suggests that analysis paralysis can be real, but that we have to increase our mental endurance in order to move past this paralysis and carry forward with meaningful action in our lives. By preparing for the outcomes and finalizing our course of action should something unexpected occur, we can ensure that we are completely ready for anything that may arise. Naturally, this advice is pretty positive if you ask me, but it took me a while to actually implement it into my life.

See, setting up plans for your "what ifs" is important, but actually standing behind those plans and seeing them through is a much bigger challenge. It's one thing to say "should *this* unexpected incident arise, I will do *this* to help me stay on track with my goals." But it is an entirely different thing when you are actually in a circumstance where you need to call on that information and put it into action, and your brain knows this.

Even though the "what ifs" of a situation rarely come into play, the fear of not knowing your alternative solution well-enough can leave you feeling unprepared and as though you are not ready to face possible challenges. Your brain becomes so fixated on the fact that you may not be truly prepared in the face of them that it attempts to use analysis and worry as a way to formulate possible outcomes to help you prepare.

Of course, most of these outcomes are heinous and involve you having something terribly horrible happen to you like you peeing your pants in front of everyone and being subjected to immense shame. But these types of intrusive thoughts are just that—intrusive. They are a form of catastrophizing that your brain uses to attempt to prepare you for every single possible outcome, even the ones that you can pretty much guarantee will never happen. I mean, I have been successfully peeing on a toilet for decades, so I can pretty well guarantee that there is no way I am going to spontaneously lose bladder control at the most inopportune time ever. But, you know, *logic*.

The best tip I have for you when it comes to preparing yourself is this: make a plan, consider the *reasonable* alternatives, and determine what you will do if those alternative situations do occur. Once you have set up your alternative plan, *accept it* and stop trying to reconsider how you may be able to improve upon it and adjust it so that you can act properly should it arise. The primary focus needs to be placed on the primary plan, as there may not be a need for you to fall back on your alternative plans. But, since you have those alternative plans at the ready, you are prepared for game day and you have nothing to worry about in the scenario where everything goes right, or in the scenario where everything goes wrong. You can still maintain your mental composure and just do the damn thing. That was a reference to my other book, *Just Do the Damn Thing*. Cough cough, wink wink, nudge nudge.

Don't Be A Whiny Little Bitch

Complaining is for pansies, no matter how you slice the cake. People who sit around and complain about their lives non-stop and never do anything to actually improve upon their lives are the worst kind of people that exist. They're the worst kind of people to be, and the worst kind of people to be around. Not only are they horribly annoying to listen to, but they are also physically rewiring their brains to focus on negativity and increase the amount of stuff they have to complain about. In other words, complaining literally fuels your content for stuff to complain about. It's simple law of attraction stuff, really.

When I was a horizontal couch potato, I was really just a whiny little bitch. Every time something happened in my life that I didn't like or that seemed inconvenient, instead of doing something about it, I would whine about it, complaining that everything bad always happened to me and that I was never able to succeed because of some reason or another. I genuinely believed that the universe was out to keep me glued to the couch and doing nothing while everyone I cared about slowly left me in the dust.

What ended up happening was just that—while everyone else was out raving about the latest concert they had gone to and their recent trip to some exotic destination and their new promotion at work, I was laying on my couch complaining that nothing good ever happened for me. My complaining got so bad that I would complain about *everything*: from the neighbor's dog barking or Netflix removing a show from their lineup that I never even planned on watching to someone driving slow on the highway. Everything was just another reason for me to complain and whine about a life that I thought was *so* horrible.

Complaining is a terrible habit that many of us cling to because it is so easy. No really, just look up "negativity bias" and you will find tons of content that tells you about our biological tendency to hold onto negative thoughts and experiences more than we hold on to positive ones. I actually talk about negativity bias in my first book, *Bitch Don't Kill My Vibe*. Wink wink, cough cough—okay, enough with the self-promotion.

Anyhoot, according to the theory of negativity bias, when we complain, we are simply feeding into the biology of our brains and refusing to take conscious responsibility for ourselves and the outcome of our negative nature. If you want to stop complaining, the best way to do it is to stop trying to run *away* from your whiny habit and start trying to move *towards* a more positive habit. In other words, instead of thinking "I'm not going to complain anymore" think "I'm going to look for more reasons to be happy in my life."

With this more positive focus, you can take clear action towards counting your blessings, increasing your feelings of gratitude, and taking account of all of the great things you have in life. Quitting the habit of complaining is not necessarily easy, but it is necessary if you are going to stop letting your pesky little mind take control and hold you back from having a happy and successful life.

"But" Nothing

"But" is one of the worst words to exist in human language. I can recall countless times where the word "but" was followed by some lame excuse as to why I was going to continue doing nothing about the things I didn't care for in my life. Absolutely nothing good follows the word "but." If you are a chronic "but" user, chances are you have a serious problem with lying to yourself and it is time to come clean about all of those times where you could have made a change *but* you didn't.

The excuses you tell yourself are probably pretty real in your own mind, but to everyone else around you, the only thing they really are is bullshit. Your excuses are just another reason as to why you are not going to make any changes in your life and why, instead of living the life of your dreams, you are going to settle for mediocrity instead. To any of your friends who have busted through their compulsive lies and found themselves on the other side of their excuse addiction, your excuses could be a serious relationship destroyer, too. That's because these are people who know that you are just telling yourself whatever it is you need to hear to justify the fact that you are lazy and unwilling when it comes to making changes in your life.

Excuses are just lies. So stop lying to yourself. Lying and cheating may have helped you win Monopoly when you were 9, but these days it will only help you stay exactly where you are—nowhere, doing nothing. It is just not worth it. If you want to stop lying to yourself and stop cheating yourself out of your dream life, you need to start by confronting what your *real* problem is when it comes to achieving the success that you desire.

Is it because you believe that you are not worthy of it? Or because you are embarrassed to admit that you want so much when you currently have so little? Is it because you were told that wanting materialistic things was frivolous and shallow and you long to be a deep, meaningful human being in the eyes of your peers? Is it because your Dad told you rich people were thieves and he never had a single good thing to say about a person with money?

The truth is, somewhere underneath your excuses is the real reason why you are unwilling to make a change in your life, and until you address it and heal that ridiculous belief, you will remain where you are and not see progress. Once you actually get into those ridiculous beliefs that have been keeping you from achieving sweet, sweet success, you need to roll back to the "What Are *You* Looking At?" section of this book and realign *your* beliefs with *your* vision.
.

Bragging on the internet can sometimes be a good thing.

This is one of those times.

Leave a review on Amazon, bragging about how awesome you are for reading this book.

★★★★★

CHAPTER 3:

CHANGE YOUR FOCUS

What you focus on grows, and for most of us, we focus on the completely negative crap about life that reminds us that we are not where we want to be. Focusing on how boring the path to success is, how much you do not want to be working right now, or how you could be doing anything else that is more enjoyable will only leave you unwilling to work towards achieving real success in your life. If you want to achieve on a high level, you need to change your focus and pay attention to the things that will actually bring you ahead in life and not the things that will hold you back.

In this chapter, we are going to discover my six favorite ideas that will help you focus your mind on the right things so you can work towards real success. These are going to increase your mental toughness so that you can stop feeling so held back by the less glamorous parts of the road to success. That way, you can actually stay on track long enough to make something of yourself.

Success Is Freaking Boring

Let me rephrase that: the road to success is freaking boring. Looking back, one of the biggest reasons I didn't start sooner in trekking towards my goals was because the mundane day-to-day tasks that are required in building success can be extremely tedious and boring. All the little to-dos and long drawn out processes necessary to get to where you want to be can be downright exhausting. It can also make you feel like you are in a tunnel where there is no end in sight.

The reality is that getting to where you want to go is not always going to be glamorous and awesome. And there are not going to be cheerleaders all along the way either. The path to riches isn't paved with gold. In fact, it's not paved at all. It's half dirt, and half made of cheap, hard to walk on, bumpy, ugly rocks, that's not pretty and that hurts when you take a step on it, so much to the point where you don't always want to take the next step. I mean, it doesn't seem like it's getting any easier or any prettier. I've got news for you, buddy. You've got to walk a long way on that not so pretty path to get to the light at the end of the tunnel—the light that you can't even see right now and are starting to lose faith of its existence. It will feel boring and it might feel completely pointless, but it's the only way to go.

Prioritizing boring and mundane tasks that lead to long term joy and success, over things that bring you joy and pleasure in the immediate moment may be challenging, especially when your friends are asking you to join them on outings and you need to be getting real work done. You may even find that you lose some friends who just don't understand why you are so devoted to doing such boring things when you could be having fun instead. I mean, at times you may feel like a complete loser who never has the chance to have fun because you are always wrapped up with something work-related. It can be tough at times. But you have to remind yourself that you're doing it so that you can get your tough times behind you.

The more you stay focused on how boring the path is, the more boring it will feel and the harder it will be for you to stay focused and dedicated to achieving real success in your life. So, you need to stop lamenting over how boring the road to success is and keep your eyes and your mind on your bigger picture. You need to consider what you are going to get out of completing those boring, mundane tasks every single day. This goes back to recalling what motivates you and using that to motivate yourself into action. If you are motivated by a fear of becoming a failure at life, remind yourself that if you do not accomplish the boring stuff, you will definitely remain a failure. If you are motivated by a future of success, remind yourself that you are only ever going to achieve your dream if you complete the boring tasks. Stay motivated, stay focused, and pay attention to what matters and the boring parts of the path to success become a lot easier to endure.

If you are really struggling with staying motivated, consider implementing a rewards system into your life. Every time you accomplish the boring and mundane tasks or a long tiresome process is completed, celebrate by doing something nice for yourself and rewarding yourself for seeing the process through. Not only will this encourage you to stay focused, but it will also help you with rewiring your brain for positivity and success. Boom. Double whammy.

Quit Tripping

I was listening to a YouTube video by Evan Carmichael about Oprah Winfrey's top 10 rules for success and one of the rules really stuck with me. That rule was that we all need to stop looking back in our lives and start looking forward towards what it is that we are creating, achieving, or working for. It sounds very simple, but most people don't do it. Oprah recalls a time when she was a really big freaking deal in the talk show scene when other people recognized her show's success and began trying to replicate it by coming out with their own inspiring talk shows. While her crew worried that their success may be trumped by the up-and-comers, Oprah maintained the same belief: we have to keep looking forward and running towards our goals because if we stop and look back, we are going to trip and fall behind.

I realized right there at that moment that I was so worried about what everyone else was doing that I never stopped to consider what *I* was doing and how my own actions were impacting my life. My constant frustration that other people were surpassing my successes or that other people were not focused enough on success became an obsession. I became so busy looking at everyone else and what *they* needed to be doing or growing angry that they were succeeding faster than I was, that I never stopped and looked at what *I* needed to be doing. This obsession stole so much of my time and positive energy that I ended up tripping big time. Not only did I trip, but I didn't even realize I had done it, so I stayed down far longer than I needed to and I couldn't get back up until I realized just how damaging my obsession had become.

If you want to achieve success in your own life, learn from my mistake and stop obsessing over what everyone else around you is doing. The ones who you believe need to be doing more are likely doing exactly what you are doing right now, and the ones you are bitter towards have no concern for people like yourself. They are too busy focused on themselves and their own success to be worried about what you believe or how you feel about them.

Any time you find yourself obsessed with someone else and "should-ing" all over the people around you, stop yourself and focus on what actually matters. Do you really think that telling other people what they *should* be doing gives you any control or supports you in achieving success? Or do you think that by considering what *you* should be doing and then actually you know, doing it, will be more meaningful towards your success? I'll give you a moment to think about it...

What You See Is Not What You Get

If you see yourself as a loser living in a cramped and uncomfortable basement suite with a crappy job and no drive or motivation, you will only ever be a loser living in a cramped and uncomfortable basement suite with a crappy job and no drive or motivation. Believing that you are the product of your environment and that what you see in your current reality is your fate will only disempower you and keep you thinking and acting small. If you want to achieve real success in your life, you need to stop basing your motivation on your current, sad reality, and start being motivated by the future visions of success that you see in your mind.

You need to become a visionary, my friend. Tap into the mind of an inventor.

Think about it: the vacuum, aluminum foil, air conditioning units, car seat covers…these were all conceptualized and created by people who refused to believe in a world where these items did not exist. They first thought about these great inventions, and then they did whatever they could to turn them into a reality, and in doing so, they created wildly successful inventions that have been used and will continue to be used by millions of people for years and years into the foreseeable future. This is what you need to do with your life. See it as a great invention and conceptualize something magnificent that you want to create out of it, even though it's not physically materialized yet. Then, begin turning those visualizations into actionable steps so that you can achieve your dream for success and move beyond this mediocre crap pile you have been calling a life so far.

A great way to start building your actionable steps is through back-tracking your success. In other words, think about the great life you want to live and reverse engineer it to uncover the steps it will take you to make that life become your reality. Create the steps starting with your vision and working all the way back to where you are at now, and then start taking action on those steps. Building your life from your dream back to where you are now is the best way to make sure that your path is designed to actually take you in the direction of your dreams. And it'll also help you keep distractions at bay, because you'll have a clear idea of where you want to go and what you need to do to get there, so you'll be able to easily eliminate distractions that may arise that can skew you off your path. Then, all you need to do is follow your designated path until you see it all the way through to your success!

Make The Big Picture Bigger

If you are the way I used to be, your mind as it is right now is not really capable of conceiving a truly big dream because you have been lying to yourself in telling yourself you believe you don't want much in life. Or, you've gotten so accustomed to mediocrity that you no longer truly believe that much more than that is possible for you. So, even the dream you may be dreaming for yourself currently could still be just as small and lame and pathetic as you are right now. Small, lame dreams are not fun or exciting and they rarely incite enough energy or motivation to inspire you to actually move into action. And they most certainly don't give you the stick-to-it-ness you need to keep trudging confidently forward when the going gets tough. Since they don't seem too far off from where you are right now in your life, they're just not that inspiring. If you want to really push yourself into action, you need to make your big dream *bigger* so that it motivates you and inspires you to move forward. If it's a little scary to you and you have no idea how you're going to make it happen, then good, that means you're headed in the right direction.

Believe me, dreaming that you will get promoted from burger flipper to burger joint assistant shift manager is not enough to get you moving. It has not gotten you moving yet, and it won't get you moving any time soon because it is far too lame of a dream. Trust me, I was trapped in that terrible dream for far more years than I am willing to admit. You need to think bigger, like, opening your own franchise or launching into a completely different industry bigger. You need to stop honing in on your simpleton dreaming and start thinking about what you *actually* want in life so that you can really inspire yourself to take action and move forward towards the success that you desire.

An activity I used to help me blow beyond my limited thinking-box and move into a dream that actually inspired me was visualization. Yep, here we are again talking about visualization. Visualization is a widely talked about yet underused tool that can actually seriously change your life, so bear with me here. Step 1: Start your visualization by releasing yourself from any judgment about visualization or the weird people who do it. Step 2: Accept that you can and will use a tool to your advantage that weird people use without actually becoming a weird person. Step 3: Release any limiting beliefs that may prevent you from allowing yourself to completely dream of the future that you desire. Then, ask yourself this one question: "what do I *really* want?" And write down what comes to mind. I recommend doing this every so often so that you can check in and make sure that you are still moving towards your real desires since our dreams have a tendency to evolve as we do.

Get Over It

We have already addressed it to some degree, but fear is a seriously limiting emotion that can hold you back from achieving anything and *everything* in your life. If I could recall the number of times that I was afraid, and let that fear turn me into a cowering fool rather than standing up and actually tackling the things that stood between me and my dream life, that number would be so obscenely large, that I'd be embarrassed to share it.

In implementing all of the other great tidbits I've offered you in this book (you're welcome), I learned one big thing about myself: I was seriously terrified of almost everything. So, I started looking into how I could begin conquering my fears and living a dreamy life that didn't involve me checking every new opportunity against my worries and phobias to make sure it was "reasonable." What I found was a great article by Ph.D. psychologist, Noam Shpancer. In his article, Shpancer states that the only way to overcome fear is to move through it so that we can see our fears all the way to the end. This made a lot of sense to me, so I began practicing it in my own life.

Instead of falling to my knees and praying for mercy from the big guy in the sky every time I experienced even an ounce of fear or trepidation in my life, I started rechanneling all of that energy and putting it into actually *facing* the fear. The best way I found for doing this was to get up and deliberately engage in anything I was afraid of in spite of fear, and commit to seeing it all the way through, which often taught me that everything I was afraid of was bullshit and it never came true anyway.

Or, if I was particularly afraid, I would use a tactic that is common in the type of therapy known as cognitive behavioral therapy, or CBT for short, for the cool people who want to sound like they know what they're talking about. This tactic is known as "playing the scene out," and requires you to continue asking yourself "and then what?" each time a new fear arises in your mind. For example, say you are afraid of skydiving because the concept of jumping out of a plane is terrifying to you. Maybe you think that when you get into the sky, you might have a panic attack and it might leave you unwilling to jump. The fear of this panic may prevent you from ever trying, thus allowing your fear to conquer you. However, utilizing the "and then what?" technique, you can use this fear as a means of supporting you in conquering your fear and conquering your mind. In this instance, if you were to ask yourself "and then what?" you might realize that either A) you overcome the panic and jump, or B) you stay on the plane and come to a landing with the pilot. Either way, you'll survive. Probably.

Allowing yourself to mentally play scenes out to the end, or simply being stubborn enough that you see things through in spite of your fears, shows you that in most cases your fears are unfounded, and you're allowing them to control and weaken your brain and destroy your confidence for no good reason really. Many times, the very things you worry about happening never actually take place.

On the odd occasion that something does go wrong, if you have done the "and then what?" technique, you will find that you are already mentally prepared to deal with anything that goes awry, or you'll come up with an alternative solution on the spot, showing you that the whole ordeal really is not as Mayday as you thought in the first place. Through these two behaviors, you will discover that your fears are rarely true, and instead, they are simply your mind trying to keep you safe from things it does not understand and from the unfamiliar.

Take The Wheel

Have you ever heard the saying "Jesus take the wheel?" This saying is usually uttered by people who feel completely defeated and who are ready to let Jesus, the Universe, God, or whatever higher power they believe in, take over control. In most cases, this saying comes after something has gone seriously wrong in their lives and they feel completely out of control so they are surrendering to whatever comes next, hoping that a higher power has a plan for getting them out of the mess they're in. While surrendering can be a valuable tool and has its time and place, you have to be careful not to use it as a crutch that prevents you from having to actually stand up and take action in your life yourself.

If you want to make real changes in your life, you need to be willing to take control over your own life and make real changes on your own account. That's right. No more blaming others and waiting around for the world to rearrange itself to work in your favor. You need to start putting forward your own action. Listen, I personally believe that whatever larger force is out there works at helping put great opportunities on our path and supporting us in moving forward in divine timing. If you are a spiritual person, you probably already believe in prayer as a powerful tool, and sometimes once you've already done all you can do in your own power, you really do have to just surrender and hope that everything works out for the best.

However, most people don't get to the point where they've honestly done everything they can possibly do in their own power. I don't believe that sitting around with your legs crossed, praying over and over for something positive to happen, as if you're Dorothy from the *Wizard of Oz*, with your eyes closed, clicking your heels, while making a wish, is going to help you achieve anything in life. You have to be willing to put forth your own efforts, too.

The best way to start taking control over your own life and receiving the right answers that you need to move forward is to stop asking "why" and start asking "how." For example, instead of saying "why is this happening to me?" say "how is this working for me?" or "how can I use this to help me improve going forward?" When you ask "why" you allow yourself to become the victim and you start giving yourself all of the answers you need to justify the fact that you are out of control and that you are a victim of your circumstances. When you ask "how," you get the answers that you need in order to move forward, because "how" is a question that is focused on finding a solution. Always ask "how," even when you are asking questions out loud. This is how you are going to begin getting solutions and actionable answers, rather than dead-end reasons or justifications that support you in feeling like an even bigger loser.

CHAPTER 4:

CHANGE YOUR HABITS

Habits are one of the biggest reasons that no one is willing (or able) to change their lives and make their goals become their reality. Our habits take complete control over our minds. When you have been committed to a habit for a long time, choosing an alternative path or finding a new way to do things and then actually sticking to that new way can be challenging. Psychologists state that it takes at least 21 days to implement a new habit, but that it can take up to around 60 days to implement a new habit that will actually stick around for the long haul. Since most people give up with their new habits in the first one to two weeks, it makes sense why so many people remain slaves to their outdated habits that keep them from ever achieving success.

For me, my habit was complaining. My routine was waking up, complaining, going to work, complaining, getting home, complaining, watching TV, complaining, and then going to sleep, while probably also complaining subconsciously in my dreams. I also occasionally fit eating, relieving myself, and some basic hygiene into that routine, all of which were also complemented with complaining. My habit was focusing on everything I didn't have or that I felt I couldn't have and it was doing absolutely nothing *for* me. The only thing my habits were good for was keeping me trapped in that unwanted lifestyle and helping me believe that I was a victim of unfortunate circumstances. In this chapter, I am going to show you how I made my brain my bitch by rewriting my habits and picking new ones that actually served me in living a better life.

Snoozing Is For Losing

Have you ever heard of the book *The Miracle Morning* by Hal Elrod? I thought it was a load of crap when friends were telling me that reading this book somehow turned their mornings into a powerful tool that helped them achieve success in their lives. I had no idea how impactful our morning actually was when it came to setting the tone for the rest of the day, and naturally, my crappy morning routine was setting me up for pessimism and failure.

So, when I heard that you could actually change your life just by changing your morning routine, I at first thought it was a bunch of bull poo. I also thought it would be way more work-intensive than it actually was, so my natural laziness kicked in and kept me a slave to my terrible, outdated excuse of a morning routine without even giving it a shot.

My original morning routine went a little something like this: wake up, complain about waking up, wallow in bed while alarm goes off, complain about how uncomfortable the shitty bed was, get out of bed, complain that I was no longer in bed, brush my teeth, complain about the crappy happenings that I predicted the day would bring, etc, etc, you get the point.

Then, I read *The Miracle Morning* for myself and discovered that there is actually a lot to be said for having a positive morning routine, and it really does set the tone for your entire day. See, most other materials I read made it sound like if your morning routine didn't include a grass and sticks smoothie, five hours of meditation, Cirque du Soleil yoga, and fish oil shots, then you were doomed to have a bad day and be worthless and unsuccessful for the rest of your life. Everything sounded so excessive and unreasonable, especially considering that at that point, I was waking up with barely an hour to spare before I started my shift at work.

When I actually read this book, however, I discovered that the most impactful part of your morning is the very first few minutes after you awake. The idea is to use those six minutes to get yourself into a positive mood that lasts throughout your entire day. So, I tried the six-minute miracle morning that was proposed on Elrod's website, and the results were incredible.
Here's how it goes:

- Minute One: Silence
- Minute Two: Affirmations
- Minute Three: Visualization
- Minute Four: Journaling
- Minute Five: Reading
- Minute Six: Exercise

A single minute for each of these activities may not seem like enough, but when I started actually putting this routine into action, I discovered that I felt *way better* than I had felt in years. I was actually excited to get up and start my day—me, the complainer—and I felt far more motivation than I ever felt when I woke up miserable and complaining about the job I had to run to in just a few minutes.

If you, like me, think that five hours of yoga and meditation is excessive, and that most food and drinks that are green are usually gross, I highly recommend trying the six-minute miracle morning. It is short, but it packs a punch and it may be just what you need to transform your mood and get your mind right in the most important moments of your morning so that you can stay mentally empowered and positive all day long.

Zip Your Lip

One of the reasons I was a horizontal couch potato perpetually covered in Cheez-it crumbs and buried under empty Oreo boxes, was that I was a bit of a people-pleaser. For you, your constant desire to gain the approval of others and mold yourself into their definition of perfect may be the very reason that you find yourself feeling unmotivated and too afraid to move forward. As a result, you may find yourself exhausted, defeated, and unwilling to do anything because it feels like you can never actually do enough or be enough to please everyone. And that is because you can't. And you shouldn't.

I can recount many different occasions where I would agree to do something I didn't want to do because it seemed like the "right thing to do," only to find myself backing out at the last minute when I realized I wasn't that interested in said activity. I just couldn't bring myself to build up the excitement, enthusiasm, or energy that I needed to actually complete these activities so I would let everyone down and back out at the last minute. Somewhere inside of me, I genuinely believed that having the intention of doing something for someone else was enough and that saying "yes" at first and backing out later on was somehow nicer than just saying "no" in the first place.

Then, after I backed out of countless events and saw the faces of disappointment and frustration (and got called out on it a time or two), I realized that I wasn't doing anyone any favors by saying "yes" when I didn't mean it. Instead, I let other people down and I made myself feel like I was weak because I could not muster up the ability and confidence to actually follow through on my word. It doesn't seem like it would be *that* big of a deal, but in the end, this vicious cycle was only damaging myself, my confidence, and causing frustrating problems for those who were learning not to trust in me or my commitments. And I was slowly learning not to trust in myself either.

Some time during my self-improvement journey, I read the book *The Four Agreements* by Don Miguel Ruiz, and the very first agreement is "Be Impeccable With Your Word." This is where I really began to understand how my lack of commitment led to me causing more problems than solutions in my own life, and how I was really letting myself and others down. So, I started following that very simple rule proposed by Ruiz: to be impeccable with my word by not making commitments that I had no intention of keeping.

Essentially, you just need to do what you say you're going to do and not do what you say you're not going to do. I started seeing every single word that came out of my mouth as a promise. I chose my words more carefully and I became a lot more cautious about the commitments I was making because I viewed the words that came out of my mouth as an obligation I had a duty to see through.

In the end, I was able to stop saying things I didn't mean and stop committing to things that didn't interest me. What followed was a series of commitments that I was willingly following through on, and a great boost to my confidence as I realized that I wasn't a useless turd and I could do things, I just had to commit to doing things that I *wanted* to do.

And the benefits extended beyond my social life being filled with things I actually wanted to do. The ancillary benefits of remaining true to my word were that I solidified my will, my drive, my persistence, my motivation and my confidence. I showed myself that I was, in fact, able to do what I set out to do. That realization made me much more mentally strong. My brain and I were now in a symbiotic relationship. I started doing what my brain told me to do, and my brain started doing what I told it to do. Applying this newfound mental fortitude to my goals made an invaluable difference in the results I began to see unfold in my life.

You're Not Going To Like This

This tip for breaking your unwanted habits and starting up new ones is one that you are not probably not going to like, but it is absolutely necessary if you want to be successful in cultivating mental toughness and changing your life. The tip is this: if you want to succeed, you *have* to start cultivating discomfort and getting used to being in uncomfortable situations, including ones that you willingly put yourself into–sort of.

See, by being brave and putting yourself into uncomfortable situations on purpose, even if you don't really want to, you improve your ability to actually get uncomfortable and manage discomfort. Naturally, the more you expose yourself to things that increase your discomfort, your understanding of how to navigate and push through discomfort and how to manage yourself in spite of these uncomfortable feelings improves.

When I first learned about this, I thought it was completely insane and that anyone who did this was nuts. I mean, who actually wants to put themselves in an uncomfortable situation and stay that way on purpose for an allotted amount of time? I mean, we have survival mechanisms for a reason, right? We have perfectly functioning instincts and mental systems in place that tell us to get the heck out of Dodge whenever things get uncomfortable for survival purposes. Aren't we supposed to crave comfort and do everything we can to stay comfortable and alive? And isn't the whole freaking point of success to be able to build a comfortable life for ourselves free of problems? The answer is: yes, it is, but getting to that point requires a lot of discomfort, and if you want to get there, you are going to have to get used to it.

One of the most influential people I have learned from when it comes to cultivating discomfort is Tony Robbins. Robbins has an empire of success, and yet he continues to build his tolerance for feelings of discomfort every single day through his cold dip pools. At every one of his 10+ houses, Robbins has a pool in his yard that is maintained at 57 degrees Fahrenheit that he jumps into and stays in for several minutes each morning. By dunking his head into the water and staying in it, he awakens his body, increases his tolerance for discomfort, and according to him, improves his ability to function throughout the day.

In addition to those cold dips, he's also a fan of cold showers. But, Robbins is also a fan of putting himself through discomfort on the opposite end of the temperature spectrum as well. He's an advocate for walking over hot coals. This discomfort doesn't stop there. He's all about sharing intimate information with strangers, yelling affirmations and "I am" statements out loud in front of other people, and facing your fears head-on. Robbins, like the new me, is a big believer in purposefully making yourself uncomfortable so that you train your mental and physical body to endure tough situations so that eventually nothing is too uncomfortable for you to handle in your life.

When Being Bad Is So Good

Your brain is a supercomputer that loves to take the lazy route to success. Despite being wildly smart and having everything it needs to easily make changes and achieve success, your brain only uses about 5% of its total capacity at any given time. The other 95% remains largely dormant or asleep while that 5% does all of the work. In that primary 5%, your brain has constructed several "loops" of behavioral patterns that it has determined as having been the most effective in helping you achieve success, whatever your current version of that is at the time. These loops become habits, and your brain effortlessly enacts them over and over again, even when they stop being the most effective method for achieving your desired future outcome.

Because of the way your brain works, it perceives anything that is outside of these habits as being "bad," even if the outside things are actually good, such as positive new habits or a new, bigger vision for yourself. For this reason, any time you attempt to introduce new habits or routines into your lifestyle, your brain will look for reasons to convince you that they are bad or that they will not work well, thus allowing it to stay lazy and operate on its primary circuits. This can lead to you staying in bad habits for a long time, all because your brain perceives them as being "good" and functional. Your brain thinks it's got things under control and if it ain't broke, don't fix it.

If you want to make serious changes in your life, you need to start rewarding your brain for engaging in "bad" behavior. Any time you engage in a new habit that your brain tries to work against or convince you of being "bad," you need to reward yourself and your brain for successfully engaging in that new behavior. You can reward yourself with a break, a treat, a new item you have been wanting to get, or anything else that supports you in seeing that engaging in this new behavior is actually a positive thing and not a bad thing.

In actively rewarding your brain for changing its behaviors, you teach it that it stands to gain more by doing the previously perceived "bad" thing than it does by doing the outdated thing that it believed was better or more efficient. As a result, you will be able to easily get your brain on board with making new habits and overriding the old ones that are no longer serving you in achieving your desired success.

Everything In Moderation

Learning that my brain was like a supercomputer intrigued me and left me wondering just what this tool between my ears is really capable of. After all, if it was capable of being so smart that it only had to use 5% of itself to succeed in keeping me alive and functional, it must be incredibly intelligent and capable of helping me succeed in many other things. One way that I learned that my brain was incredibly powerful was when it came to overcoming challenges and powering through things that I previously thought were impossible. This ultimately meant that I was overcoming my default desire for procrastination. See, I used to think that being challenged in life meant that I was stupid or incapable and that I would never amount to anything because I lacked the skills to achieve whatever it was that I needed to do.

That's how intelligent my brain is: that it can actually trick me into consciously believing that I am incapable when the reality is that it is just too lazy to actually do anything uncomfortable or outside of its ordinary to do list. My brain is really just trying to keep me alive, so, to my brain, everything is just fine as long as it is being fed and exercised on a regular basis. Since depriving my brain of food and forcing it to comply through deprivation wasn't an option, I decided that learning how to activate the other 95% and force it to do things it didn't want to do would have to suffice. So, I went on to learn how I could teach my brain to stop valuing doing things that would keep it comfortable, thus forcing the other 95% to kick in and shake things up.

For me, a big part of this tied into overcoming procrastination. One way of doing that, which may initially seem counterintuitive to doing things that make you uncomfortable, is to create designated times where we do what makes us feel good. The idea is to basically take smaller steps in achieving success, and put boundaries on our procrastination. Try giving yourself five minutes to engage in fun activities that would normally be distractions that would cause you to struggle to pay attention to your necessary task at hand, and then as soon as the five minutes is up, get straight back to work for a designated period of time of perhaps an hour or so, whatever your attention span will allow, as long as your work time is significantly longer than your break time.

By putting boundaries on my distraction time, adding structure to my work time, breaking down the tasks I needed to do thus making them easier to manage, and incorporating more of what I enjoyed, it became a lot easier to keep my brain on board with working towards the big picture. Because it wasn't constantly getting bored and losing focus to other seemingly more interesting and fun things, it was easier to keep myself focused, embrace new habits, and get done the things

I ultimately needed to get done to get me closer to my goals.

Maybe You're A Little Special...

Remember how I said you're not that special? Well, that's not *entirely* true. See, you are not so special that everyone spends all of their time thinking of only you, but you *are* special in the sense that you have a unique gift that comes more easily to you than it does to other people. And that unique gift also usually happens to be of value to others around you, but my main point is this: By understanding your special gift, you can use it to build up your confidence and leverage it to help you create and maintain new positive habits and achieve success.

You can do this by taking advantage of keystone habits. Sometimes, it can be overwhelming to think of the idea of having to muster up the mental strength to start a million new habits. If your life is so far off track that you find it completely and utterly overwhelming to even hold on to the *idea* of starting a bunch of new habits, try just picking one keystone habit to focus on. A keystone habit is a habit that has positive effects that trickle down into multiple areas of your life and can automatically trigger other good habits without you having to consciously work at them. The result is that you end up with a slew of good new habits, and a heck of a lot of newfound confidence in yourself, which will make your brain much more resilient overall.

For instance, if you focus on the habit of working out every day, in order to make that habit happen, you may have to wake up an hour earlier each day to have time to get your workout in. And you may have to eat healthier because whenever you try to work out with a belly full of sausage McMuffins, it just doesn't…work out. And you may have to skip watching two hours of TV every night because you need to go to bed early enough to have the energy to work out the next morning. And you may have to quit smoking because as it turns out, it's quite difficult to work out with lungs full of emphysema. So, while you set out to only conquer one habit, you have inadvertently conquered five new habits without even realizing it. Figure out what you're good at, and develop a keystone habit around it.

Instead of placing all of your focus on ditching bad or unwanted habits, you're putting your focus on increasing positive and wanted habits. I did this early on by identifying that I was incredible at getting motivated and starting new endeavors, but I was not necessarily the best at following them through. So, instead of focusing on how terrible I was at follow through, I focused on how great I was at motivating myself into action. Then, by learning how to motivate myself, I was able to build momentum that led to me ultimately getting my ass off the couch and making some serious changes in my life. All of those changes ended up landing me right here, writing this book and sharing my life-changing tips with you so that you, too, can change your own life. When you focus on what you are good at, what you are good at magnifies and you become great at a whole lot of things. All you have to do is adjust your focus, focus your energy, change your habits, and watch your entire life change before your very eyes.

You also might find the added bonus that focusing on what you're good at can have a reciprocal ripple effect in helping both others and yourself. For example, say you're naturally good at giving pep talks and inspiring other people to do better in their lives. You could leverage this skill and increase your own positivity by giving more pep talks and improving your capacity to inspire people by reaching out to inspire even *more* people. As a result, this leveraging could have a ripple effect into your entire life, supporting you in staying positive yourself and living a better life overall. If you are being more positive to and for other people in your life, you will start feeling more positive and inspired in your own life.

And you never know, it could lead you even further. As you reach out to connect with and inspire even more people, you may even find a hidden talent, passion, or opportunity that you had no idea existed previously that you can now tap into and leverage to help you move forward with an even greater impact and to an even greater degree. Through that, you may discover your dream career path, and then, as you follow that path, everything on your vision board may just come true. Tap into your inner snowflake and find what's unique about you. Following that can have a massive ripple effect and impact on your life and the lives of others for the better.

CHAPTER 5:

CHANGE YOUR ACTIONS

You can't always rely on your unconscious habits (whether good or bad) to do all the work for you. Sometimes, you have to make deliberate thoughts, decisions, and actions to help move you forward in life. Until now, it is likely that many of the actions you have taken in your life are backed by pesky little habits like negative self-talk, poor self-confidence, or your commitment to staying comfortable. However, not every single action you make is a habit and so, when you arrive at new decisions, you need to know how to consciously take action in your life and move forward intentionally and successfully in the right direction. In this chapter, I'm going to show you how I was able to stop making weak decisions at every turn and start taking bold, confident and focused action in my life.

Here We Go Again

If you have been trapped in a habit loop that has kept you making the same terrible decisions over and over again, it's time for you to take responsibility for your choices and make a change. In other words, you need to skip over your habits and start making decisions to take new action. It's time for you to learn your lesson and move on so that you can stop being dragged down by the same nonsense that has kept you down for so long already.

For me, the guilty pleasure that constantly kept me down was my diet. Hanging out on the couch watching Netflix and lounging my life away wasn't really conducive to positive eating decisions. I would consistently munch on unhealthy processed snacks, eat takeout, and skip over meals in favor of sitting down and staying comfortable instead. But in a way, I wasn't actually comfortable at all. I started gaining weight, I never actually felt *good*, and I was struggling to really make any significant changes in my life. My increasing weight and decreasing stamina left me feeling embarrassed, especially since I struggled to do basic things like walk and talk without feeling winded. Truth be told, I was at my lowest point when it came to health at the time and I was feeling really bad about myself. I knew I needed to make a change, but I couldn't seem to keep motivated or feel disciplined enough to actually stick to those changes or even make the first step. Lounging around and eating pizza or Chinese food was just so much easier than looking up a healthy recipe, going to the grocery store to get ingredients, and then cooking to make a healthy meal for myself. So, I stayed uncomfortable, unhealthy, and unhappy as I just repeated the loop over and over again.

When I decided to start making changes for myself in my life, one of the first changes I knew I needed to make was around my diet. I realized that if I was ever going to feel better, look better, and have the stamina to keep up with the people in my life, I would need to start choosing healthier food options and get some regular exercise into my daily life. Of course, nothing changed until I actually consciously decided to make a change by adjusting my diet and eating something different. I had to throw away all the junk food, order a nutrition plan from a nutritionist online, empty out my fast food coupon drawer, and delete all my favorite take-out spots from speed dial on my phone. Yeah, I was in deep. But none of it happened without action. Deliberate action to stop playing that same sad record on repeat.

Chances are, if you look into your own life, you can also find areas where you have been paying the consequences for the same repetitive behaviors, but refusing to actually take action to make a change so that you can see improvements in your life. If that is the case, you need to start looking at what these lessons may be and discovering how you can learn from them and begin implementing them into your life so that you can stop facing the same consequences over and over again. As they say, if you want to experience something different, you have to do something different. If you continue on with the behaviors that you have been using until now, nothing will ever change and you will always find yourself struggling to see the improvements that you desire to see because you are not taking the necessary actions in order to make those improvements a reality in your life.

Look In The Mirror

Have you ever looked at the people in your life as mirrors? Have you ever considered the people in your life as reflections of yourself? The relationships that you have in your life could very well directly reflect the relationship you have with yourself, giving you a clear look into who you are and how you truly feel about the person that you have become in your life. If you are like I was a few years back, that may completely terrify you when you notice that the relationships in your life are toxic, meaningless, or completely non-existent. In fact, you may even do as I did and completely reject this reality until one day you are looking in the mirror and you make the connection by realizing that your relationship with yourself really sucks.

The closer you are with people in your life, the more they will reflect you to yourself and give you a clearer picture of how you truly feel about yourself and the relationship you share with you. If you lack any close, intimate relationships in your life or if the ones you do have are in shambles, chances are you don't feel too hot about yourself, and the relationship you share with yourself is not a positive one. You may find yourself avoiding close relationships or rejecting them because somewhere deep inside you realize that these people expose you to yourself in ways that you do not like. Or, you may find yourself clinging to them and wishing for them to work out, while allowing these relationships to become damaging or destructive and tear you down from any success you may stand to achieve.

If you notice that your relationships suck and you can't seem to keep close friends in your life no matter how hard you try, chances are you need to do some serious work on your relationship with yourself. The best way to do this is to get in front of a real mirror with yourself and start saying everything that you wish someone else would say to you, including the corny stuff or the things that make you feel ashamed. For example, if you need reassurance about how important you are and the value you bring to relationships, reassuring this to yourself in the mirror is a great place to start. This will help you stop looking outside of yourself for approval and comfort and strength, while also helping you start seeing yourself as whole and worthy.

When you begin to improve the relationship you share with yourself by telling yourself everything that you need to hear (all the good things, that is), you will discover that your capacity to improve the relationships you share with others is increased, too. This is because you are no longer leaning on other people, waiting for them to complete you and help you feel whole because you already feel whole and complete on your own. Once you build up an inner strength and foundation of confidence, you'll be able to take that steady, unshakeable mental state with you everywhere you go and in everything you do.

Chill Out, Bro

People who desire to be resilient and possess more mental strength probably want to do so because they ultimately want to get to work on becoming something bigger and better than they already are. After all, you don't need mental strength and confidence to just remain the same. That's probably why you picked up this book, I'm guessing. But, as much as jumping into action and getting to work are necessary when it comes to changing your life, you also need to know how to slow down and engage in complete and total relaxation on a regular basis. Balance, people, balance.

In fact, one of the leading problems that results in people remaining unwilling or unable to move forward in life is burnout or total mental exhaustion from having to balance or think about far too many things at once. Has your head ever hurt from just thinking too hard? I remember right before I said "screw it" and took my horizontal hiatus, my people-pleasing, lack of self-confidence, and apparent inability to do anything right despite repeated attempts resulted in me feeling extremely burnt out and unwilling to do anything more. I wasn't making progress in my life because at that time, I couldn't. Over time, the "I couldn't" became "I wouldn't" and I refused to move forward or do anything because I realized it was much easier to keep myself out from under serious pressure than it was to expose myself to it again and risk another serious burnout.

Of course, at that time, my short-sightedness lead me to falsely believing that there was no way I could possibly avoid burnout and that any level of action would certainly leave me overly exhausted and overly frustrated. But, around the time I started asking "how?" instead of "why?" I discovered that one key change I could make moving forward was knowing when to slow down, and slowing down in a way that was timely and effective. In other words, I needed to know how I could completely relax at the end of every single day and wind down so that I was not carrying the day's stresses into the next day and the next and the entire rest of my life. In being able to completely release from my day, I was able to get a great nights' rest and wake up ready to tackle another new day with mental clarity and confidence.

I started implementing a simple night time routine that was as easy as my six-minute Miracle Morning routine by Hal Elrod. I realized the importance of both starting off your day and ending your day right. Starting your day deliberately and well primes your day for optimum results after your morning routine is over. And ending your day deliberately and well primes your day for optimum results the following day.

The night routine I created for myself was easy:

- Journal
- Meditate
- Breathe in fresh air
- Engage in one super relaxing thing for a half hour that allowed me to completely de-stress from the day

My half hour of relaxing "me time" would sometimes consist of me watching an episode of my favorite comedy show or reading a fiction book. Other times, it would be taking a hot shower or soaking in a hot tub. Whatever I intuitively feel that I need in order to completely relax at the end of each day, I do it, and I do it with my fullest possible attention.

Sometimes, life gets really hectic and we need a skosh more than a nightcap to get us through the chaos and stress. For those times, I recommend having an arsenal of powerful relaxation tools that you can call on to help you completely let everything go. Your more extreme arsenal may include things like going out and getting a massage or spending a weekend in a cabin, or taking a long hike in nature. Having something you can call on to help you chill the F out will ensure that you are always locked, loaded, and ready for those especially challenging seasons in life. Just make sure that when you're engaging in your relaxation techniques, you also set the intention to fully commit to them and engage in them completely. That means being fully present in every way—physically, mentally, and emotionally.

The trick to getting a mental recharge is to not mentally be in two places at once. You can't be getting your Woosah on in a candlelit jacuzzi while going through your phone reading all the unread emails you have from today and wracking your brain with your to do list for tomorrow. And it's not only bad to let work get in the way of your zen time. It's just as bad to let your personal life interfere. Let your relaxation time be *your* relaxation time. Don't succumb to the pressures of responding to text messages or calls from family and friends. Your friend doesn't need to know *right now* what you think of the outfit they're planning on wearing to their date next weekend. Your mom doesn't need to know *right now* what you're planning on bringing to potluck Thanksgiving next year. They can wait. It's 30 minutes. Take advantage of it and use it strictly for you and you alone. Remember, a clear mind is a strong mind and a strong mind is a clear mind. So don't let your stress build up too much in favor of getting things done or running around attempting to please and answer to other people in your life, because that will only lead to burn out, frustration, a weak mind, and a desire to quit on your way to achieving great things in your life.

What On Earth Do You Mean?

Some people believe that every single person is born with their own divine purpose that they have been put on Earth to fulfill. Others believe that we create purpose in our lives by choosing something meaningful to us and fully engaging in it in a meaningful and heart-filled manner. Whichever side of the coin you're on doesn't mean anything and doesn't matter, but just know that you do need to land on one side or the other, rather than bumbling around in your life aimlessly with no purpose. That's the most surefire way to end up being a weak minded quitter because you have nothing driving you forward and no real, strong enough reason to keep going.

People who attempt to go through life without any purpose or meaning end up depressed and haggard. They are either doing nothing at all, or constantly half-ass pursuing a better life but never have anything really pushing them along and mentally helping them achieve that "better" life that they dream of having. Without this driving force, it's impossible to be resilient and remain mentally strong in tough times. Staying devoted to any one thing is virtually impossible when everything you attempt to devote yourself to is so wildly out of alignment with who you are and what you desire to achieve in your life. If you haven't already figured it out, you need to discover why you're here on this Earth and how you plan on making an impact with this one life that you have been given.

If you run any form of business or if you have ever looked into the idea, chances are you have heard the saying: "your business is only as meaningful as your why." In other words, the reason *why* you are in business is more important than almost any other aspect of the entire business. If your reason for running the business is not strong enough, your ability to run your business is going to falter and you will find yourself quitting the moment things get tough. You will not have what it takes to withstand those tough seasons and so, to put it simply, you won't. Instead, you will fail, sit down, and resort back to sofa butt-ruts and Cheez-It crumbs.

This ideology does not only apply to business, but it also applies to your life. Attempting to move forward in your life without any meaning or purpose is only going to leave you feeling unmotivated and unwilling to continue forward any time things grow difficult. You need to have a meaning or purpose in your life that you can keep top of mind any time the going really gets tough. Because without it, trust me, the tough will not be able to get going.

When you are looking to discover what your life purpose is, it is important that you look within you and discover what would give your life a sense of meaning in a way that actually matters to you. Cross-check your purpose against your values and see if it truly fits with who you are and what you care about in this life, or if it is just a whim that you are following because you thought you might be able to make it matter to you if you just tried a little bit harder. Picking things that genuinely mean something to *you* will be the most effective way in naturally keeping you interested and focused when it comes to building a life that you love.

Avoid picking a purpose just because it sounds good or because you think other people will admire you more for it. These purposes are often shallow and rarely have any real meaning to you. Sure, saving the whales sounds good and deep and all, but if you don't actually want to save the whales but are saying that you do just to try to look good in front of other people, then your "good" and "deep" purpose all of a sudden becomes bad and shallow.

According to Oprah (my favorite person on Earth), "There is no greater gift than to honor your life's calling. It's why you were born, and how you become most truly alive." I would have to strongly agree with her. One, because that's true, and two because even if it wasn't, it still would be true because everything she says is right in my eyes. Since discovering my own life purpose and realizing that my existence has significant meaning in this life, I have discovered that I have far more to offer than I ever believed I did back when I was too busy lounging around on the couch bitching about my misfortunes that I was doing absolutely nothing about. Furthermore, I am actually excited and inspired by each new morning and ready to embrace each new day with that inspiration, more so than I ever was before I knew what my purpose in life truly was.

You're A Joke

When was the last time you laughed? And I mean a good, deep from the pit of your belly, so loud that you're embarrassed, stomach hurts, head hurts laugh? I am going to go out on a limb here (for the sake of making my point) and say that for you, it's been a while. In fact, you may even be willing to secretly admit to yourself that it has been years since you laughed so hard that you thought you might pee your pants because it was just that deep and genuine.

You may think that laughter is for the weak, for the people who don't take things seriously enough. I mean, it kind of makes sense. Laughing is sort of the opposite of being serious. When we think of mental toughness and resilience and strength and confidence, it usually conjures up images of Marines, the military, frowns, stoic faces, furrowed brows, abnormally and uncomfortably erect posture, and yelling whilst making pretty much no facial expression. But, you may be surprised to know that laughter is a wonderful form of medicine that is actually known to increase your mental toughness and resiliency so that you can continue moving forward in life without taking everything so personally or allowing everything to keep you down.

Getting a good laugh in on a regular basis is not only enjoyable, but it will actually provide you with proven mental health benefits that will help you break through a rut and get into a new phase in your life. According to my good friends Dr. Lee Berk and Dr. Stanley Tan at Loma Linda University in California (okay, they're not actually my good friends, but they are doctors), laughing is known to reduce your stress hormone levels and support you in ditching feelings of anxiety. This may be why your body subconsciously responds with out-of-place laughter when you are experiencing extreme levels of fear or anxiety in your life. Ever laughed at a funeral, anyone? Just me? Getting laughter into your daily routine, or at least getting a good laugh in once or twice a week, can help you reduce the amount of stress you feel in your body and help you feel happier overall.

So, you may be thinking, "Wait a minute, I just got a book on mental toughness and they just told me laughter is the best medicine?" Yes. But that's not all. You have to take it a step further. Actual laughter is not the only positive type of laughter that you can engage in to your mental benefit. Perhaps more importantly, you need to learn how to laugh things off when you make a mistake or when things don't go your way. Don't take your screw ups so seriously. That's how you convince yourself to stop dead in your tracks instead of forging ahead.

Learning to see things with a humorous perspective is known to help people cope with challenging circumstances and experience a greater resiliency towards challenges that may present themselves. When you laugh at yourself after experiencing something frustrating, embarrassing, or inconvenient, you increase your mental resiliency and support yourself in coming back from this challenge without experiencing too significant of a stress increase from it. It won't be easy to make you feel defeated and want to give up. As a result, you will be able to carry on with your day and with your plan and with your life without having the weight of stresses, mistakes, and temporary defeats dragging you down.

I remember when I was sitting on the couch in my rut, after a long stint of…well, nothing, but I was watching *Brooklyn 99*, which is a pretty funny show overall, but I was in such a funk in my life that I couldn't even really laugh or enjoy it. But, eventually, about 15 minutes in, I couldn't hold it in anymore. Adam Samberg said something so hilarious and I started laughing as if I was all of sudden making up for not having laughed in months—which, I kind of was. To this day, I have no idea where that laughter came from or what inspired me to just go with it, but I do remember that following my laughter felt incredible. I didn't stop myself, I just let it run. It was like getting a good cry in and letting all your emotions out in an emotional catharsis, except I was laughing for what seemed like forever, getting it all out. As I wiped away the tears from my eyes and caught my breath, I realized it had been an incredibly long time since I had enjoyed a good, full laugh. From that day on, I realized that Adam Samberg is one of the greatest comedic actors of our time. Oh, and I also realized that I needed to have the ability to laugh off things that don't go my way and accept them for what they are. I can honestly say, this tip has been life-changing for me.

If you have a difficult time laughing or if you feel like you are genuinely not able to get into a full fit of laughter, I recommend making this a priority in your life. Watch great comedies, or go see one live, and let yourself fully immerse into the experience without letting yourself be distracted by other thoughts or pressures from the rest of your life. If stand-up comedy isn't your thing, watch funny cat videos on Youtube or go out with your funniest friends (everyone has at least one funny friend) and do your best to have a carefree night where you fully engage in the conversation and let yourself really laugh. Do everything you can to truly engage in full, exaggerated laughter, and watch how just one bout of laughter completely transforms your mood and, as a result, your perspective on all of the problems that you currently face in your life. Life is just easier when you're happier.

Who's To Blame?

When things aren't going your way and your life doesn't look how you want it to look, it's easy to blame everyone around you. But are they really the reason you are where you are? Are they really the reason why you are not taking action towards achieving your goals *right now*? For me, I was constantly blaming everyone and everything for why I was unable to do anything to get myself out of my rut and I was hellbent on defending why nothing was ever my fault. I blamed my Mom for not teaching me better when I was growing up, my neighbor for being too loud so I couldn't sleep, my boss for being too mean so I couldn't perform, and my friend for being too needy so I couldn't take time to work on myself. I blamed my dog for needing to go to the bathroom and requiring time and attention from me, and I blamed the weather for why I couldn't be bothered to dress nicely. Literally anything I could blame to excuse myself from having to take responsibility for my shit life, I did. I was constantly playing the blame game as a way to avoid the fact that there was only one reason why I was not doing better than I was in my life, and that reason was little old me.

See, when you don't let yourself take responsibility for things in your life, it becomes easy to justify why you are a lazy pile of bones camped out on the couch for months on end. When you blame others, you mitigate the responsibility, and therefore give yourself permission to give up on everything. Because, hey, it's not your fault you suck at life because nothing is in your control anyway, right? Wrong. Victim mentality is for the weak. Sure, sometimes your pathetic little charade can cause nice people to take pity on you and do nice things for you to try and help you out during your slump. Of course, once those nice people realize that you are abusing the blame game for your own personal gain, they disappear and will likely never come back into your life again because, newsflash buddy, you are not disadvantaged, you are just lazy.

Blaming everyone else seems like a great way to win mentally in the short term because it feels good, but if you really want to win at life in the long run and conquer your mind, you need to be willing to take responsibility for everything in your life. *Everything.* In doing so, you empower yourself and give yourself the ability to take back control and make the necessary changes to actually make something of yourself. That's because when you take responsibility, you stop waiting for everyone else to change their behaviors or "pay" for their contribution to your shitty situation and you start taking charge your damn self.

Despite what anyone else may have contributed to your current circumstances, if you're going to get ahead, you have to refuse to be held down by how you think other people wronged you, and instead let it motivate *you* to do better in *your* life. This is *your* life. Are you really going to let it stagnate and come to a screeching halt because you're so held up on not getting past what you think someone else did to wrong you? Especially when that someone else has probably long forgotten about what they did or stop caring or never even realized they did anything against you in the first place?

Now, to be serious for a moment, there are of course varying degrees of betrayal and some people have endured unspeakable traumas that have been inflicted on them by other people, but in the most respectful, empathetic, and loving way possible, I have to tell you: Get over it. No matter how hard it may be. No matter how justified you are in knowing that someone did something wrong to you. It doesn't mean that the other person is right. And it may take therapy. But, I, as your friend (can I assume that we're friends now?), want you to reach your greatest potential and live your best life. But your only chance at still having the life you deserve is to put certain things behind you and do what you can do from here on out to create *your* life into what *you* want it to be despite what has happened to you or what other people have done to you in the past.

In fact, a message that really hit home with me was one shared by the late, great self-development author and speaker Wayne Dyer, where he said: "take responsibility for your part, even in the situations you felt were beyond your control." As an example, let's say you were abused or mistreated by a partner and you struggle to get motivated to change your life because the abuse you endured was painful and left you with deep emotional and mental wounds. At the end of the day, you need to take responsibility for only two things in order for you to change your life: your willingness to let someone else abuse you for the time that it went on, and the lasting wounds you are left with now. It doesn't make the other person a good person. And it doesn't make you a bad person. It doesn't mean that they are right. And you are wrong. It's just about taking responsibility for the parts that you can so that you can move onwards and upwards with strength.

In certain situations, your willingness to allow certain things to happen to you may feel completely beyond your control in the heat of the moment, but often it only feels that way because you are blinded by the emotion and fear that arises within you. However, at the end of the day, there are often many solutions that can support you in making a change in your life and getting out of almost any sticky situation you may find yourself in.

Then, once you are out, you need to take responsibility for the fact that even though it was not you who damaged yourself, it is you who needs to clean up the pieces and move forward. Blaming the other person only works for so long before it eventually becomes your own problem because you are not willing to make necessary changes in your life so that you can heal from the pain. This may sound backward or even painful, harsh, or insensitive, but I say it in your best interest. You need to find a way to take responsibility for everything in your life if you ever plan on healing from damage or trauma and rebuilding a positive life for yourself.

Team Up

You are only in charge of your own life, and the only life that you are seeking to improve at the end of the day is your own. However, this does not mean that you need to proceed all by yourself or that you are an island who cannot ever reach out for support or gain the benefits of connecting with other humans in your life. In fact, it's recommended and even necessary if you really want to begin building a better life for yourself. Remember that African proverb about going further together? Well, we're coming back and making a whole section on it now because it's that important. This whole teamwork thing seriously matters if you want to truly take control and begin making positive changes so that you can live a better life and heal from your lazy, ineffective ways.

Having people in your life and learning how to nurture the relationships you share with these people is a great way to begin building up a more positive relationship with yourself. As you learn to treat other people you have friendships and relationships with in a healthy and compassionate manner on an ongoing basis, you will also learn how to treat yourself in this positive way.

Another reason why relationships are positive and necessary, and what I think is the actual meaning behind the proverb, is that people have the capacity to offer you support, guidance, and knowledge that you will not always have yourself, and vice versa. Mentors and coaches can show you the shortcut to success, but even just having a positive, healthy relationship with people in your life in general can help you feel connected, appreciated, worthy, and accepted in your life. Having these basic needs of feeling important and valuable supports you in feeling more confident in achieving things on your own in your life and can bolster your mental strength in times of weakness. And with a firm foundation of solid relationships, you know that making a mistake or even failure will not result in you being completely isolated, mocked or tarred and feathered by people who do not actually care about you or your feelings.

I'm going to be honest with you, if you have been isolated for quite some time, you might have a hard time rebuilding old friendships or developing new friendships in your life. You may have been spending the last several months telling yourself that you are a horrible friend because you haven't felt energized enough to communicate with your existing friends or agree to go hang out with them. Or, you may feel too embarrassed to go out with your friends or meet new people because when the inevitable "What do you do?" and "What's new?" or "What have you been up to?" questions come up, you're ashamed that you don't have anything meaningful or impressive to say.

Because of this, you may feel like none of your friends like you or want to reach out to you anymore, or like you are a burden on them and that you don't deserve their friendship. If you experience these types of thoughts, I suggest you go back through this book and apply some of the tips to friendship, such as the tips about changing your mind. Allowing yourself to rewrite your beliefs around friendship and your deservingness when it comes to having friends will help you realize that just because you have made some withdrawn decisions in the past does not mean you are suddenly unworthy.

You still deserve to have positive friendships and chances are that most, if not all, of your friends still believe the very same thing and still want to hang with you. Chances also might be that they have been mentally and emotionally going through some of the same struggles that you have, but just haven't been open with talking about it or haven't allowed it to adversely affect their lives the way it has for you. When you are rebuilding your relationships with them, do not let your past experiences define the friendship that you are re-cultivating. Be clear and honest with your friends about how you have been feeling and where your headspace has been. And don't apologize for being human. All humans go through tough times. But should you choose to apologize for your absence in the relationship, accept that when they accept your apology, they truly have forgiven you. There is no need to continue "repenting" for being a "bad friend" for the past while.

If you find that you are in the market for new friends because your old friends have been gone for so long or no longer fit into your new life, you might struggle to really put yourself out there for fear of not being worthy. I'm here to remind you that just because you have been a lazy sack on the couch for the past several months or even years (I don't know your situation and I'm not judging), does not mean that you are not worthy or capable of having positive friendships in your life. You do not have to lead with stories about how flaky you were or how bad of a friend you were to people in your past. You are not some form of dangerous offender who needs to lead with a warning and a disclaimer when going into any new relationship or friendship. You are just a human who went through a hard time and who needs to accept that hard time and allow yourself to emerge back into the real world with confidence and the willingness to remain open to what comes next while putting your past behind you.

CONCLUSION

Hey, look at you! You made it all the way to the end of this incredible book about making your brain your bitch and changing your entire life in the process. (Can I toot my own horn and call my own book incredible? I just did.) How does it feel knowing that you just made a commitment to yourself to sit through the duration of an entire life-changing book? As an added note, the secret to life changing books, however, is that they kind of only work *after* the book is over, when you apply the information by taking action in your actual life.

But, the very fact that you have made it all the way to the end here proves that you are serious about wanting to change your life and create it into something that's not so embarrassing to talk about at high school reunions. I'm incredibly proud of you for your dedication and commitment, but moreover, *you* should be incredibly proud of yourself for devoting time and energy to your own personal growth and development.

It may not seem like a lot right now, but the very fact that you are willing to take your commitments seriously means that you are ready to stop being a mental wuss and start taking some real action in your life.

Those dreams you have been daydreaming about in private all along, they are about to become your reality if you stay on this path and continue moving towards creating real, meaningful success in your life. In order to stay on this path, you have to give up your "go with the flow," "woe is me," "nothing ever works out for me" attitudes for good and start taking control over your mind and your life every single day, one action at a time, one habit at a time, one thought at a time. No more sitting around on the couch letting things happen to you as you pretend you don't care or pretend that your life being in shambles is not having a negative impact on you. No more butt ruts! It's time to get up and take responsibility for everything and recognize that when you don't like something in your life, it is your responsibility (and yours *alone*) to change it.

In order for you to take this information with you and make it really stick, I encourage you to pick three of your absolute favorite techniques from this book and make a commitment to begin applying them right away. These do not necessarily have to all be from the same chapter or in chronological order. It would be ideal to choose tips from different chapters so that you can get more well-rounded results from your efforts, since each chapter focuses on a different general area. Then, continue practicing your three tips until they become second nature to you. Think about them, refine them, reflect on how they are changing your life, continue to implement them, and adjust your strategy to improve your implementation. But only start with three tips at first. Once you have really mastered applying these three tips to your life, choose three more to tackle next. You can keep going in this way until you have successfully implemented and mastered every single strategy that you feel fits with your life and your life goals, and until you've become a lean, mean, success machine.

By taking your time and implementing your strategies slowly and intentionally, you ensure that you are not going to attempt to throw yourself into a brand new life altogether only to find yourself retreating back into your old habits just days later due to overwhelm. Believe me, I cannot tell you the number of times I bit off way more than I could chew and set out to become a completely different person within 24 hours by trying to completely redesign my entire life in a single day. I wanted to be able to show people how impressive I was and how I was open and flexible when it came to making the necessary changes in my routine so that I could live a better life overall. I wanted to be able to show myself how quickly and easily I could turn my life around. But instead, I ended up trying to change so much at once that I could not maintain any of the changes and I backslid into my old, outdated habits. In the end, I was so embarrassed by my inability to progress or make a change that there came a point where I never bothered to tell anyone about my intentions anymore. I was afraid that if I told anyone about the exciting new life I was setting out to create, I would just screw up again, backslide into the old me, revert back to wearing socks with sandals, and have all of my previous failures replaying in my head, setting myself up for disapproval, disappointment, and mockery from the finger-pointing "I told you you couldn't do it" crowd.

So, instead of publicly sharing my commitments, eventually, I started to privately keep them to myself and make them quietly without telling anyone. In the end, when the benefits of my new habits kicked in and I was able to stick with moving towards my new intentions for my life, the work I was putting in started working and the results spoke for themselves. Everyone could very easily and obviously tell that I was no longer that loser covered in Cheez-It dust, stuck in the butt ruts on the couch. I was able to move out of that crappy cardboard box I once called home, put my own home-cooked meals on the table, and begin seeing success living a life I was excited about and saw purpose and meaning in. I was no longer committed to my struggle. Instead, I was committed to my success.

Now, I'm going to tell you right now so you can't come back whining to me when everything doesn't fall into place within the first five minutes of you finishing this book. *But you made it sound like it was easy*—No. No, I didn't. I will tell you right now. It is freaking hard. Changing your habits, changing your life, changing the wiring in your brain, changing your mentality, changing your beliefs, changing your default mental state, forcing your brain and your body to do things you know they should do but they don't want to do, saying no to fun nights out in favor of boring nights in hustling alone towards your goals, learning to truly believe in yourself, learning to never give up, cultivating positive self talk, changing what has been ingrained in you your entire life up to this point that has gotten you to where you are now…It. Is. Hard. It is going to suck.

Starting is going to be hard. The very first step is going to be hard, let alone consistently implementing these tips and staying completely devoted regardless of whether you "feel like it" or not until you see lasting results. At times, you are going to find yourself cursing under your breath at how challenging it is, cursing out loud at *me* at how challenging it is, or denying how bad your life really is, so you can try to convince yourself you don't *really* need to make these uncomfortable changes in your life. You may also find yourself struggling to look at yourself and feeling a deep sense of shame and embarrassment for how bad you have let your life get, or how harsh you have been to yourself without even realizing it. Believe me, I know how challenging these things are to face. I was in your exact position just a few years ago, maybe even worse. It is all going to be one big suck…until it's not. If you keep at it, it will be worth it.

If you are willing to stay committed to your journey, focus on the results that you stand to gain (or the failure that you stand to avoid), and keep moving forward, you will find that your entire life changes in less time than you think. In the beginning, when making change is hardest, it's going to feel like it's taking forever. But as you get into the swing of things, one day, you'll look back and that old version of you will feel so distant, and it will be so hard for you to remember even being that person.

The best way to change your life is to make subtle, consistent shifts over a long period of time. This is no get-rich-quick, get-successful-quick, turn-into-an-amazing-person-overnight scheme and you are not going to find yourself completely healed from your laziness and inner challenges before it's time for your next meal. However, you are going to find that with consistent and committed action, change happens a lot faster than you think. With a little bit of hope and a whole lot of implementation, you stand to transform your life from being a sad, pathetic, direct-to-DVD story that you hide from people out of shame and embarrassment, to a Hollywood blockbuster that you are proud for everyone to see. In no time at all, you will be holding your head high and your shoulders square, shaking people's hands and introducing yourself as the incredible lion or lioness that you truly are, roaring in people's faces. Maybe not the roaring. But, you, my friend, are the king or queen of your very own jungle, and that is an incredibly badass thing to be.

Remember, you are not a victim, and the Universe has not set out to destroy you or prevent you from living your fantasy life as it seemingly hands everyone else the key to their dreams. You are just someone who for whatever reason has not yet taken full responsibility for themselves or tapped into the 95% of your brain that is ready to serve you, but that secretly keeps itself hidden away in the shadows of your mind. By implementing the techniques in this book, you are going to be able to access that incredible power and begin living your very best life. Leave your victim mentality completely behind and get ready and excited for what is to come. It will be completely worth it, trust me.

Lastly, if you enjoyed this book and feel empowered to take control over your own life, I ask that you please consider leaving a review on Amazon and Audible. Your feedback is greatly appreciated. Hearing your opinion and understanding how my own (hopefully) inspiring experiences and understandings may help you improve your own life is valuable in helping me to continue producing great content to support you in living your best life, and it just makes me smile inside to see that I was able to somehow have a positive effect on someone else's life with my antics.

Thank you, and I wish you the best of luck in achieving your best life. I know you have it in you to make your brain your bitch. You can do this! I promise. I believe in you. Now go on out there and *ROAR* in the face of your challenges and show your brain and your life who's really in charge. Your dream life awaits you, and you are more than ready to grab the bull by the…horns…and make that dream life of yours a reality. See you at the top.

Like what you just read?
Sad it's over?
Turn that frown upside down
and listen to the audiobook
(~~usually $14.95~~)
for **FREE**.

audible
an amazon company

Search for my name
"Reese Owen" on Audible.

Audible member? Use a credit.
New to Audible? Get this audiobook **free**
with your free trial.

ALL BOOKS BY REESE OWEN

Check out my other ebooks, paperback books, and audiobooks available on Amazon and Audible:

B*tch Don't Kill My Vibe
How To Stop Worrying, End Negative Thinking,
Cultivate Positive Thoughts,
And Start Living Your Best Life

Just Do The Damn Thing
How To Sit Your @ss Down Long Enough To
Exert Willpower, Develop Self Discipline,
Stop Procrastinating, Increase Productivity,
And Get Sh!t Done

Make Your Brain Your B*tch
Mental Toughness Secrets To Rewire Your Mindset
To Be Resilient And Relentless, Have Self Confidence
In Everything You Do,
And Become The Badass You Truly Are

CPSIA information can be obtained
at www.ICGtesting.com
Printed in the USA
BVHW041859130521
607292BV00012B/481